Better partnership working

MANAGING AND LEADING IN INTER-AGENCY SETTINGS

Better partnership working

Series editors: Jon Glasby and Helen Dickinson

About the authors

Helen Dickinson is Associate Professor of Public Governance at the School of Social and Political Sciences and Melbourne School of Government, University of Melbourne, Australia. Her expertise is in public services, particularly in relation to topics such as governance, commissioning and priority setting and decision-making, and she has published widely on these topics. Helen is co-editor of the *Journal of Health, Organization and Management* and the *Australian Journal of Public Administration*. Helen has worked with a range of different levels of government, community organisations and private organisations in Australia, the UK, New Zealand and Europe on research and consultancy programmes.

Gemma Carey is Senior Lecturer and National Health and Medical Research Fellow with the University of New South Wales, Australia. She has published widely on different aspects of public administration and public health. Gemma's monograph on joined-up government and public administration with Melbourne University Press was published in 2015 – *Grassroots to government: Joining-up in Australia* – and she was chief editor and contributor to *Designing and implementing public policy: Cross-sectoral debates*, published by Routledge in 2016.

MANAGING AND LEADING IN INTER-AGENCY SETTINGS

Helen Dickinson and Gemma Carey

Second edition

First edition published in Great Britain in 2008, reprinted 2009, 2010

This edition published in Great Britain in 2016 by

Policy Press
University of Bristol
1-9 Old Park Hill
Bristol BS8 1SD
UK
t: +44 (0)117 954 5940
pp-info@bristol.ac.uk
www.policypress.co.uk

North America office:
Policy Press
c/o The University of Chicago Press
1427 East 60th Street
Chicago, IL 60637, USA
t: +1 773 702 7700
f: +1 773 702 9756
sales@press.uchicago.edu
www.press.uchicago.edu

© Policy Press 2016

British Library Cataloguing in Publication Data
A catalogue record for this book is available from the British Library

Library of Congress Cataloging-in-Publication Data
A catalog record for this book has been requested

ISBN 978-1-4473-2984-8 paperback
ISBN 978-1-4473-2986-2 ePub
ISBN 978-1-4473-2987-9 Mobi

Cover design by Policy Press
Printed and bound in Great Britain by Lavenham Press Ltd, Suffolk
Policy Press uses environmentally responsible print partners

Contents

List of tables, figures and boxes

Tables

Figures

Boxes

Acknowledgements

Helen and Gemma would like to acknowledge the contribution of a number of people who have allowed them to draw on and use their work in this book. Special thanks go to Edward Peck who was the first author of the original version of this text. Although a new role and time constraints sadly prevented Edward from contributing to this revised version of the text, parts of his original contribution remain, which he has kindly allowed Helen and Gemma to use.

Helen and Gemma would also like to acknowledge Paul Williams for allowing them to draw extensively on his excellent work on boundary spanning. They would also like to thank Perri 6 and colleagues (Table 1.1 and Figure 1.1), Keith Grint (Figure 1.2), Siv Vangen and Chris Huxham (Figure 2.1), Jean-Louis Denis, Ann Langley and Viviane Sergi (Figure 3.2), Brenda Zimmerman and colleagues (Figure 4.1), Mark Exworthy and Martin Powell (Figure 4.2), and Doug Easterling and Judith Millesen (Table 4.5) for allowing them to reproduce their work. Finally, their thanks also go to George Cox for his assistance in the final stages of the book in terms of formatting and bringing together references.

Any personal opinions (or errors) in the book are those of the authors alone.

List of abbreviations

Health and social care use a large number of abbreviations and acronyms. Some of the more popular terms used in this book are set out below:

CCG   clinical commissioning group
CCT   compulsory competitive tendering
DH   Department of Health
JCB   joint commissioning board
LSP   local strategic partnership
NHS   National Health Service
NPG   new public governance
NPM   new public management
ODPM   Office of the Deputy Prime Minister
OECD   Organisation for Economic Co-operation and Development

All web references in the following text were correct at the time of printing.

Preface

Whenever you talk to people using health and social services, they often assume that the different agencies and professions talk to each other regularly, actively share information and work closely together. Indeed, most people don't distinguish between 'health' and 'social care' at all – or between individual professions such as 'nursing', 'social work' or 'occupational therapy'. They simply have 'needs' that they want addressing in a professional and responsive manner – ideally by someone they know and trust. How the system is structured behind the scenes could not matter less.

And yet, people working in health and social care know that it *does* matter. None of us starts with a blank sheet of paper, and we all have to finds ways of working in a system that was not designed with integration in mind. As the books in this series explain, different parts of our health and social care services have evolved over time as largely separate entities, and policy-makers, managers and front-line practitioners trying to offer a joined-up service will typically face a series of practical, legal, financial and cultural barriers. This is often time-consuming and frustrating, and the end result for service users and their families often still does not feel very integrated (no matter how hard the professionals were working to try to produce a joint way forward). As one key commentator suggests, 'you can't integrate a square peg into a round hole' (Leutz, 1999, p 93).

When services aren't joined-up, it can result in poor outcomes for everybody – gaps, duplication and wasted time and resources. People using services frequently express amazement at the number of different people they have to tell their story to. Instinctively, it doesn't feel like a good use of their time or of the skilled professionals who are trying to help them. Often, one part of the system can't do something until they've had input from another part, and this can lead to all kinds of delays, inefficiencies and missed opportunities.

For staff, it can be surprisingly difficult to find enough time and space to gain a better understanding of how other agencies and professions operate, what they do, what priorities they have and what constraints they face. For someone who went into a caring profession to make a difference, there is nothing more dispiriting than knowing that someone needs a joined-up response but not knowing how to achieve it. In many situations, workers feel they are being asked to help people with complex needs, but with one hand constantly tied behind their back.

For the broader system, this state of affairs seems equally counter-productive. If support is delayed or isn't sufficiently joined-up, it can lead to needs going unmet and to people's health rapidly deteriorating. It then becomes even harder and even more expensive to intervene in a crisis – and this leaves less time and money for other people who are becoming unwell and need support (thus creating a vicious cycle). Poor communication, duplication and arguments over who should pay for what all lead to inefficiency, bad feeling and poor outcomes for people using services. In extreme cases, a lack of joint working can also culminate in very serious, tragic situations – such as a child death, a mental health homicide, the abuse of a person with learning difficulties or an older person dying at home alone (see Box 0.1 for but one high profile example). Here, partnership working is quite literally a matter of life and death, and failure to collaborate can have the most serious consequences for all involved.

Box 0.1: Partnership working as a matter of life or death

Following the tragic death of Peter Connelly (initially known as 'Baby P' in the press), Lord Laming (2009) was asked to produce a national review of progress since his initial investigation into the equally horrific death of Victoria Climbié in the same borough of Haringey (Laming, 2003). As the 2009 review observed (Laming, 2009, para 4.3):

> It is evident that the challenges of working across organisational boundaries continue to pose barriers in practice, and that cooperative efforts are often the first to suffer when services and individuals are under pressure. Examples of poor practice highlighted to this report include child protection conferences where not all the services involved in a child's life are present or able to give a view; or where one professional disagrees with a decision and their view is not explored in more detail; and repeated examples of professionals not receiving feedback on referrals. As a result of each of these failures, children or young people at risk of neglect or abuse will be exposed to greater danger. The referring professional may also be left with ongoing anxiety and concern about the child or young person. This needs to be addressed if all local services are to be effective in keeping children and young people safe.

For health and social care practitioners, if you are to make a positive and practical difference to service users and patients, most of the issues you face will involve working with other professions and other organisations. For public service managers, partnership working is likely to occupy an increasing amount of your time and budget, and arguably requires different skills and approaches to those prioritised in traditional single agency training and development courses. For social policy students and policy-makers, many of the issues you study and/ or try to resolve inevitably involve multiple professions and multiple organisations. Put simply, people do not live their lives according to the categories we create in our welfare services – real-life problems are nearly always messier, more complex, harder to define and more difficult to resolve than this.

Policy context

In response, national and local policy increasingly calls for enhanced and more effective partnership working as a potential solution (see, for example, DH, 2013). While such calls for more joint working can be inconsistent, grudgingly made and/or overly aspirational, the fact remains that collaboration between different professions and different organisations is increasingly seen as the norm (rather than as an exception to the rule). This is exemplified in a previous Welsh policy paper, *The sustainable social services for Wales: A framework for action* (Welsh Assembly Government, 2011, p 11) that argued, 'We want to change the question from "how might we cooperate across boundaries?" to justifying why we are not.' With most new funding and most new policy initiatives, there is usually a requirement that local agencies work together to bid for new resources or to deliver the required service, and various Acts of Parliament place statutory duties of partnership on a range of public bodies. As an example of the growing importance of partnership working, in 1999 the word 'partnership' was recorded 6,197 times in official parliamentary records, compared to just 38 times in 1989 (Jupp, 2000, p 7). When we repeated this exercise for the first edition of this book, we found 17,912 parliamentary references to 'partnership' in 2006 alone (although this fell to 11,319 when removing references to legislation on civil partnerships that was being debated at the time). Since then, there have been two general elections/new governments and a series of major spending cuts and pressures – arguably making joint working harder to achieve in practice, but even more important.

In 1998, the Department of Health issued a consultation document on future relationships between health and social care. Entitled *Partnership in action*, the document proposed various ways of promoting more effective partnerships, basing these on a scathing but extremely accurate critique of single agency ways of working:

> All too often when people have complex needs spanning both health and social care good quality services are sacrificed for sterile arguments about boundaries. When this happens people, often the most vulnerable in our society ... and those who care for them find themselves in the no man's land between health and social services. This is not what people want or need. It places the needs of the organisation above the needs of the people they are there to serve. It is poor organisation, poor practice, poor use of taxpayers' money – it is unacceptable. (DH, 1998, p 30)

Whatever you might think about subsequent policy and practice, the fact that a government document sets out such a strongly worded statement of its beliefs and guiding principles is important. How to move from the rhetoric to reality is always the key challenge – but such quotes illustrate that partnership working is no longer an option (if it ever was), but core business. Under the coalition government (2010-15), this previous language shifted once again – and most recent policy refers to the importance of 'integrated care' (rather than 'partnerships' or 'collaboration'). As the coalition's NHS Future Forum (2012, p 3) argued:

> Integration is a vitally important aspect of the experience of health and social care for millions of people. It has perhaps the greatest relevance for the most vulnerable and those with the most complex and long-term needs. We have services to be proud of, and patients in England already receive some of the most joined-up services in the world. However, too many people fall through gaps between services as they traverse journeys of care which are often too difficult for them to navigate themselves. This lack of integration results daily in delays and duplication, wasted opportunities and

patient harm. It is time to "mind the gaps" and improve the experience and outcomes of care for people using our services.

While it is not always fully clear what a commitment to more integrated care might mean in practice (see below for further discussion), recent policy seems to be trying to achieve a number of different things, including:

- greater *vertical integration* between acute, community and primary care
- greater *horizontal integration* between community health and social care
- more effective joint working between *public health* and local government
- more effective partnerships between the *public, private and voluntary sectors*
- more *person-centred care*, with services that feel integrated to the patient.

In response to all this, the time feels right for a second edition of this book and of our 'Better partnership working' Series more generally. While our overall approach remains the same (see below for a summary of our aims and ethos), key changes to this edition include:

- updated references to current policy and practice
- the addition of more recent studies and broader literature
- a greater focus on 'integrated care' under the coalition government (2010–15) and the Conservative government of 2015-
- new reflective exercises and updated further reading/resources
- updated 'hot topics' (with a particular focus in some of the books in the series on the importance of working together during a time of austerity).

Aims and ethos

Against this background, this book (and the overall series of which it is part) provides an introduction to partnership working via a series of accessible 'how to' resources (see Box 0.2). Designed to be short and easy to use, they are nevertheless evidence-based and theoretically robust. A key aim is to provide *rigour and relevance* via books that:

• offer practical support to those working with other agencies and professions and to provide some helpful frameworks with which to make sense of the complexity that partnership working entails;
• summarise current policy and research in a detailed but accessible manner;
• provide practical but also evidence-based recommendations for policy and practice.

Box 0.2: The series at a glance

• *Partnership working in health and social care* (Jon Glasby and Helen Dickinson, 2nd edn)
• *Managing and leading in inter-agency settings* (Helen Dickinson and Gemma Carey, 2nd edn)
• *Interprofessional education and training* (John Carpenter and Helen Dickinson, 2nd edn)
• *Working in teams* (Kim Jelphs, Helen Dickinson and Robin Miller, 2nd edn)
• *Evaluating outcomes in health and social care* (Helen Dickinson and Janine O'Flynn, 2nd edn)

While each book is cross-referenced with others in the series, each is a standalone text with all you need to know as a student, practitioner, manager or policy-maker to make sense of the difficulties inherent in partnership working. In particular, the series aims to provide some practical examples to illustrate the more theoretical knowledge of social policy students, and some theoretical material to help make sense of the practical experiences and frustrations of front-line workers and managers.

Although there is a substantial literature on partnership working (see, for example, Hudson, 2000; Payne, 2000; Rummery and Glendinning, 2000; Balloch and Taylor, 2001; 6 et al, 2002; Glendinning et al, 2002; Sullivan and Skelcher, 2002; Barrett et al, 2005; Glasby and Dickinson, 2014a, for just some of many potential examples), most current books are either broad edited collections, very theoretical books that are inaccessible for students and practitioners, or texts focusing on partnership working for specific user groups. Where more practical, accessible and general texts exist, they typically lack any real depth or evidence base – in many ways, they are little more than partnership 'cookbooks' that give apparently simple instructions that are meant to lead to the perfect and desired outcome. In practice, anyone who has studied or worked in health and social care knows that partnership working can be both frustrating and messy – even if you follow the so-called 'rules', the end result is often hard to predict, ambiguous and likely to provoke different reactions from different agencies and professions. In contrast, this book series seeks to offer a more 'warts and all' approach to the topic, acknowledging the realities that practitioners, managers and policy-makers face in the real world.

Wherever possible, the series focuses on key concepts, themes and frameworks rather than on the specifics of current policy and organisational structures (which inevitably change frequently). As a result, the series will hopefully be of use to readers in all four countries of the UK as well as other national settings. That said, where structures and key policies have to be mentioned, they will typically be those in place in England.

While the focus of the series is on public sector health and social care, it is important to note from the outset that current policy and practice also emphasises a range of additional partnerships and relationships, including:

- broader partnerships (for example, with services such as transport and leisure in adult services and with education and youth justice in children's services);
- collaboration not just between services, but also between professionals and people who use services;
- relationships between the public, private and voluntary sectors.

As a result, many of the frameworks and concepts in each book may focus initially on public sector health and social care, but will also be relevant to a broader range of practitioners, students, services and service users.

Ultimately, the current emphasis on partnership working and on integration means that everything about public services – their organisation and culture, professional education and training, inspection and quality assurance – will have to change. Against this background, we hope that this series of books is a contribution, however small, to these changes.

Jon Glasby and Helen Dickinson
University of Birmingham and University of Melbourne
December 2015

1

What are management and leadership, and why do they matter in collaboration?

Over the past century ideas derived from management, and more recently leadership, have become ubiquitous concepts in our everyday lives. There are countless books and articles that deal directly with these issues, and you would struggle to browse in a bookshop for more than a few minutes without finding several books on these topics. Flick through any newspaper, or watch any TV channel, and stories are invariably underpinned by discussions of responsibility and accountability. When an organisation – or groups in society more broadly – encounters difficulty, it almost invariably looks towards some form of individual leadership to guide it through the time of turbulence or to take the blame for failing to do so. Typically, media and public attention focuses on the person at the top who is presumed to have both the authority and the acumen to intervene to make things better. As has been argued elsewhere, 'the "organisation in our heads" is still heavily influenced by the principles of classical management theory' (Anderson-Wallace, 2005, p 171), which assumes hierarchical relationships between members of a single organisation. Yet the reality of the modern world is a proliferation of collaborative arrangements, where the important leadership activities are those that take place between a range of different partners. This poses significant challenges for traditional concepts of leadership and management, and is the focus of this book.

The number and range of public sector collaborations has grown considerably since the mid-1990s. Rather than collaborative working being an additional activity for public sector agencies, arguably it is now 'the new normal' (Sullivan, 2014). The expectation is that collaborative working will enable public services (and their voluntary and private sector partners) to better address the 'wicked' problems of society, and, as suggested in Box 0.1, 'better' partnership working has also frequently been suggested as a way of preventing avoidable deaths and improving the quality of lives for vulnerable individuals and their families. These expectations are frequently as much aspirational as plausible. This is understandable. Politicians and policy-makers usually want to persuade the public – and the latter often want to be persuaded – that new innovations in public services will deal with complex, troubling and perhaps irresolvable social problems (for further examination of this important theme, see Dickinson, 2014). Stern and Green (2005) describe what could reasonably be called a spirit of collusive over-optimism that infuses many local agency descriptions of their collaborative arrangements. Sullivan et al (2004, p 1610) suggest that 'the need to justify their existence to unpredictable national funders means that localities have become adept at laying claim to impacts in all sorts of areas.'

Despite management and leadership being possibly some of the most written about phenomena of the past 50 years, the evidence base is far from conclusive (Peck and Dickinson, 2009), and the evidence relating to management and leadership within inter-agency settings is complex, contradictory at times, under-theorised in some areas and theoretically dense in others. As Chapman et al (2015, pp 15-16) argue, 'even though there has been an increase in scholarship on multi-sector, collaborative and network environments of public administration ... it has not translated to more published articles about leadership in these types of settings.' This new edition is substantially revised as a reflection of the developments in the broader literature. In addition to updating the policy context and including new publications and evidence, we have incorporated a new set of hot concepts and emerging issues in Chapter 3, and a range of new helpful frameworks and concepts in Chapter 4.

What is clear from the literature that has emerged since the previous edition over the past eight years is that, although leading across boundaries appears to be more important than ever before for public and private organisations alike, there are no easy answers. As we will see in the pages that follow, leading and managing across inter-agency settings involves complex processes that require that close attention be paid not just to individual leaders and managers, but those individuals and groups that are (or might be) followers and the contexts that these activities are performed in. In this revised edition we have scoured the literature to draw out the most useful aspects of the evidence base, and present it in a way that is accessible for manager, practitioner and student audiences alike. At times the concepts explored are challenging, but the intention is that this nuanced account should more accurately reflect the myriad of situations that leaders and managers of collaborative endeavours find themselves encountering.

This chapter starts by considering why management and leadership have gained such prominence within the collaboration literature, before going on to consider a certain set of individuals (commonly known as 'boundary spanners') who have become central within these debates. We then outline the many forms that collaborative activities may take, and the implications this has for discussions of management and leadership of inter-agency initiatives. The following section provides a brief overview of the paradigm of new public management (NPM), the influence this has had on public policy over the past 30 years and implications for readers of this book. One consequence of NPM has been increased interest in networks, and the link between collaboration and networks is considered here, along with the emergence of a more recent theory – new public governance (NPG). The final section considers current major theories of management and leadership in order to provide some clarity about the nature of management and leadership in inter-agency settings. Having set out the contours of the conceptual literature in this chapter, we then move on to consider what the research evidence tells us in the following chapter.

Why is collaboration not always successful?

When we wrote the first edition of this book we noted that there was a lack of evidence to demonstrate that attempts at collaboration had clearly illustrated improvements in outcomes for those who use services. Despite significant and ongoing investment in this field, eight years on we find the picture is largely the same (this is explored in more detail in the introductory book in this series by Glasby and Dickinson, 2014b, and also in *Evaluating outcomes in health and social care* by Dickinson and O'Flynn, 2016). To some extent we should not be entirely surprised by this. It is difficult to find a figure that is agreed on, but general research from the commercial sector suggests that over 40% of alliances fail and more still are plagued by under-performance (Tuch and O'Sullivan, 2007; Zollo and Meier, 2008). The overwhelming message from this literature is that mergers and acquisitions rarely succeed in delivering anywhere near the promised payoffs (Field and Peck, 2003).

Some years ago now Kanter (1989) wrote about her understanding of the North American private sector, suggesting that a failure to adequately manage collaborations might be responsible for the poor outcomes reported in respect to joint initiatives. We would argue that this is a perspective that still holds strong in the literature today. Kanter pointed to research indicating that while managers spend up to 50% of their time initiating collaborative arrangements and a further 23% of their time developing strategic collaboration plans, they spend only 8% of their time actually managing collaborations. Yet, when collaborative attempts do not live up to their lofty expectations, one of the factors often cited as being responsible for their failure is lack of leadership, or inappropriate management. Given this analysis it may well be that leaders and managers are not focusing on the 'right' kinds of factors that actually drive collaborative relationships.

As Kanter notes, the challenge of leading and managing inter-agency collaborations is a more difficult task than operating in traditional hierarchical organisations where, she argues, the former may lack a common framework between partners; exhibit asymmetrical power relations (that is, one partner holds more power than the other/s); possess incompatible values; have unclear authority and communication channels; and deploy different professional discourses. Of course, these latter three characteristics, at least, may also be present in well-established and apparently hierarchical public service organisations. Nonetheless, Kanter's analysis does start to map out the contours of the particular terrain that has to be negotiated by those managing and leading in inter-agency settings and the dilemmas this produces. Herranz (2008, p 2) describes this as a situation where 'public managers face the quandary of being expected to work more in networks where they have little authority, while at the same time increasingly being held more accountable for performance and improved outcomes.' This mismatch between authority and accountability is one we will return to a number of times in this chapter and the broader book.

Echoing some of Kanter's themes, UK health and social care collaboration has tended to bring together organisations characterised by different accountability regimes, priorities, values, institutional rules, roles and rituals, diverse financial cycles and so on. As long ago as the early 1990s, Hardy et al (1992) produced a list of barriers to collaboration between health and social care that still resonate today (see Box 1.1), despite this analysis being based on relationships in place before the introduction of either the purchaser–provider split or extensive private sector involvement in healthcare. Again, this list may contain items that could also characterise individual organisations (for example, fragmentation of responsibilities within agency boundaries and professional self-interest); nonetheless, there are themes here to which we need to return in considering the particular challenges of managing and leading in inter-agency settings.

Box 1.1: Barriers to collaboration in health and social care

Structural

- Fragmentation of service responsibilities across inter-agency boundaries
- Fragmentation of service responsibilities within agency boundaries
- Interorganisational complexity
- Non-coterminosity of boundaries

Procedural

- Differences in planning horizons and cycles
- Differences in budgetary cycles and procedures

Financial

- Differences in funding mechanisms and bases
- Differences in the stocks and flows of resources

Professional

- Differences in ideologies and values
- Professional self-interest
- Threats to job security
- Conflicting views about user interests and roles

Status and legitimacy

- Organisational self-interest
- Concern for threats to autonomy and domain
- Differences in legitimacy between elected and appointed agencies

Source: Hardy et al (1992)

Evidence for the positive impact of collaborative activities, then, is scarce given the significant investments and the plentiful accounts of challenges (see, for example, Cameron et al, 2012; Dickinson, 2014). Some organisations have sought to overcome difficulties in creating inter-agency collaboration by appointing individual managers – network coordinators, integrated service managers, joint commissioning managers – to glue these entities together. It is presumed that these post holders will solve the problems created by these various obstacles where they can (and negotiate a way around them when they cannot). As a result, McCray and Ward (2003, p 362) suggest collaborative working is all too often 'the action of a few individuals with vision that have created change in service delivery in relation to people's lives and opportunities. These individuals have managed to work and lead effectively despite the maze of separate service budgets, distinct disciplines and different values.' In other words, in everyday practice, individual managers – and their leadership skills – are viewed as essential in making collaboration work (to the extent that they can or do work). In the broader organisational literature, these individuals are usually known as 'boundary spanners'.

Boundary spanners

The literature on collaboration has long focused on individuals who engage in boundary-spanning tasks, processes and activities, although as Williams (2012, p 32) notes, 'there is a considerable degree of conceptual confusion about the term and an absence of definitional clarity that must be addressed.' Boundary spanners go by a number of different and often quite strange names within the literature, such as *linking pins, boundroid, input transducer* (Leifer and Delbecq, 1976), *reticulists* (Friend et al, 1974), *strategic brokers* (Craig, 2004) and *entrepreneurs of power* (Degeling, 1995). In the broad array of individuals who are described as boundary spanners, Williams (2012) argues there are two major categories. The first comprises individuals who have a dedicated role in working in multi-organisational/multi-sector settings. This group is small in number in the context of the overall public service workforce. The second group comprises those managers, leaders and practitioners who undertake boundary-spanning activities as a function of their role. It is this latter group that we most closely focus on in this book.

In the next chapter we provide a more detailed discussion of the research on leadership and boundary spanning. In the remainder of this section we establish the basic aspects of the concept. In defining who boundary spanners are and what work they do in inter-agency settings, Williams (2012, p 58) identifies four major roles: reticulist, interpreter/communicator, coordinator and entrepreneur (see Table 1.1). He goes on to argue that there are particular competencies associated with these roles, and there is a 'high degree of connectivity and interplay between the role elements and competencies' (p 60). An adapted version of these roles and competencies is outlined in Table 1.1, and it is important to note that some, if not all, of the characteristics identified by Williams as common to boundary spanners might also be recognised as fundamental in all organisational managers (in particular in the more 'transformational' and 'post-transformational' models of

Table 1.1: Roles and competencies of boundary spanners

Role	Dominant images	Main competencies
Reticulist	Informational intermediary, gatekeeper, entrepreneur of power	Networking, political sensitivity, diplomacy, bargaining, negotiation, persuasion
Interpreter/ communicator	Culture breaker, frame articulator	Interpersonal, listening, empathising, communication, sense-making, trust-building, conflict management
Coordinator	Liaison person, organiser	Planning, coordination, servicing, administration, information management, monitoring, communication
Entrepreneur	Initiator, broker, catalyst	Brokering, innovation, whole systems thinking, flexibility, lateral thinking, opportunistic
Learning and connecting	Stewardship, cultural broker, knowledge broker	Building knowledge of policy networks, bridging skill and knowledge gaps in how to work in relational environments

Source: Adapted from Williams (2012 p 58)

leadership that have emerged over the past decade; see below for further discussion).

Collaborative form and implications for management and leadership

Of course, also crucial to the formulation of effective management and leadership is the nature of the collaboration within which it is being exercised. There are numerous frameworks that seek to categorise collaboration (see, for example, Hudson et al, 1998; Leutz, 1999; Ling, 2002, Peck, 2002), each of which draws on different sorts of factors such as the number of partners, what links partners and the nature of these relationships. It is argued that these factors are important as they tell us about the nature of the context in which leaders and managers are operating and the sorts of rules that govern activities. Within the academic literature three ways of thinking about organisational relationships are often presented: hierarchies, markets and networks. As discussed in Glasby and Dickinson in this series (2014b), a hierarchy is a single organisation with top-down rules, procedures and statutes that govern how the organisation works. Market relationships involve multiple organisations exchanging goods and services based on competition and price. A network is often seen as lying in between these two approaches, with multiple organisations coming together sometimes more informally and perhaps voluntarily, often based on interpersonal relationships or shared outlooks or outcomes (Thompson, 1991; 6 et al, 2006). Rodríguez et al (2007) have caricatured these approaches as being about rules (hierarchy), incentives (market) and interactions (network).

Collaboration has often been equated with the network form, given the focus on horizontal relationships. Yet collaboration can take any one of these different forms. Hierarchical forms have tended to dominate public services; even where markets and networks have become more prominent in recent years, they are typically new ways of handling relationships between hierarchies. This is, in part, because markets in the public sector are largely (if not exclusively) 'quasi-market' arrangements, requiring ongoing steering and management by government. In a study of the prevalence of collaborative public management in the US, McGuire (2006, p 40) notes:

> [F]ar from being episodic or occurring in just a few programmes, collaboration in public management is as common as managing bureaucracies, and even more so in such areas as economic and community development, the environment, energy management, and the entire gamut of social and human services. It is important to recognise that bureaucracy is not going away; collaboration still complements, rather than supplants, single organisation and management.

Today we more often find 'hybrid' arrangements rather than the disappearance of hierarchical forms (Crouch, 2005). As Brandsen et al (2005, p 750) explain, 'empirically speaking, it appears far easier to find arrangement that are hybrid or "fuzzy arrangements".' In thinking about health and social care collaboration, we will inevitably be considering a range of different forms of relationships between partners, and therefore a number of different approaches to leadership and management. Moreover, some of these collaborations will be obligatory (think of youth offender teams) or encouraged to transform into new forms of hierarchy (think of community mental health teams) or asked to operate in a market (think of joint commissioning boards [JCBs] or clinical commissioning groups [CCGs]) (for a more detailed discussion, see Glasby and Dickinson, 2014b).

Some commentators have identified these relational forms with specific periods of recent history: 1940s-1970s, hierarchy; 1980-1990s, markets; and post-1997, networks. Although misleading in many respects, this approach links discussions of networks to one of the most important ideas in organisational writing over the past two decades: new public management (NPM). We give a short overview of NPM because of its importance to the prevalence of, and enthusiasm for, networks (and also for the popularity of the division in public services of commissioning from providing which has accompanied the trend towards networks). It is also an important concept in explaining the enthusiastic rise of management and leadership over the past 30 years. In more recent years the movement of new public governance (NPG) has emerged in response to NPM, and we briefly reflect on this and its implications for leadership and management of contemporary public services.

New public management

In 1995, the Organisation for Economic Co-operation and Development (OECD) observed that 'a new paradigm for public management has emerged, aimed at fostering a performance-oriented culture in a less centralised public sector' (1995, p 8). The paradigm referred to is new public management (NPM), which is essentially founded on a critique of hierarchy as the organising principle of public administration (Dunleavy, 1991); it is argued that the top-down decision-making processes associated with this model are increasingly distant from the expectations of citizens. The case goes that, while the commercial sector had undergone radical change in the 1980s, the public sector remained 'rigid and bureaucratic, expensive, and inefficient' (Pierre and Peters, 2000, p 5). This explains why NPM is often seen as the application of private sector management techniques to the public sector. Of course, many in the public sector have stressed the significant differences between the two sectors and thus the inappropriateness of such an application (see, for example, Carnevale, 2003).

Various advocates differ in their descriptions of NPM (Pollitt, 1993; Hood, 1995; Ferlie et al, 1996). In general, however, it is characterised as an approach which:

- emphasises establishment and measurement of objectives and outcomes;
- disaggregates traditional bureaucratic organisations and decentralises management authority;

- introduces market and quasi-market mechanisms;
- strives for customer-oriented services.

Osborne and Gaebler's (1993) popular text *Reinventing government* is a prominent example of the NPM paradigm. It sets out 10 main principles for reforming the public sector in order that it might become more aligned with a commercial sector ethos (see Box 1.2). While written more than 20 years ago the principles set out still reflect many of the themes and trends that we see in government reform around the world today.

These principles contain significant implications for the way that public sector organisations are managed and led. Indeed, the benefits of NPM are often described in contrast to the drawbacks of 'old public administration', where the latter is characterised by the diplomatic maintenance of organisations that are inward looking and which have been designed and are run in the interests of the professional staff who work in them (Harrison et al, 1992). From another perspective, Lynn (2006, p 142) describes this approach as being 'governed by rules and hierarchy, and by the public service values of reliability, consistency, predictability, and accountability', highlighting the value of bureaucratic structures even if they may not always be perfectly efficient (Graeber, 2015). NPM, on the other hand, favours managers and leaders who are, for instance, customer-focused and entrepreneurial. Of course, this is an over-simplistic dichotomy; nonetheless, in these circumstances, the enthusiasm for the transformational model of leadership in public services since the late 1990s (see below) is easier to understand.

Box 1.2: Ten principles for 'reinventing government'

1. *Catalytic government:* steering, not rowing.
2. *Community-owned government:* empowering rather than serving.
3. *Competitive government:* injecting competition into service delivery.
4. *Mission-driven government:* transforming rule-driven organisations.
5. *Results-orientated government:* funding outcomes, not inputs.
6. *Customer-driven government:* meeting the needs of the customer, not the bureaucracy.
7. *Enterprising government:* earning rather than spending.
8. *Anticipatory government:* prevention rather than cure.
9. *Decentralised government:* from hierarchy to participation and teamwork.
10. *Market-orientated government:* leveraging change through the market.

Source: Osborne and Gaebler (1993)

As Lawler (2000, p 33) describes, the introduction of new managerialism stressed

> ... the role, power and accountability of individual managers and accentuates their positions as managers, rather than as administrators, officers or senior professionals. Accountability for success or otherwise lies at the door of each individual manager, operating within strategic guidelines and being responsible for the achievement of organisational objectives.

Growing pressures for economic and social change in the 1990s saw interest in the management of public services being superseded by a focus on 'highly effective leadership and a requirement for new leadership skills' (PIU, 2001, p 11). Martin and Learmonth (2012, p 281) describe how 'leadership has become a term of choice among policymakers, with positive cultural valences which previously predominant terms such as "management" now lack.' We return later in this chapter to the differentiation between management and leadership, but the point remains that in recent years we have seen somewhat of an obsession with the power of 'leadership' in public services.

Many of the major reforms of health and social care over the past 30 years can trace their roots back, at least in part, to ideas derived from NPM – from the introduction of general management in the NHS and compulsory competitive tendering (CCT) of goods and services, which up to this point were provided by local authorities in the 1980s, through to the purchaser–provider splits of the 1990s, to the plurality and choice agenda of the 21st century. For our present purposes, one of the key consequences of NPM needs highlighting, which is connected to the first of Osborne and Gaebler's principles (see Box 1.2): *governments should steer, but not row*. Underpinning this tenet is the argument that if public sector bodies concentrate on *what* should be delivered (and the performance management of outcomes), they will do so more efficiently if they are not preoccupied with the details of *how* this should be delivered. This shift, of course, has profound implications for the activities of leaders and managers.

Implications of new public management for public sector management and leadership

Over the past 25 years many public services have ceased to be provided by the NHS and local authorities (or by government more widely in many different geographical jurisdictions; see Alford and O'Flynn, 2012), and have been transferred to a wide variety of agencies (for example, private companies providing domiciliary care, voluntary bodies proving community-based drug and alcohol services, arm's-length maintenance organisations providing housing services, NHS foundation trusts providing mental healthcare). This has led to a proliferation of providers, many of which are markedly different in their origins, incentives and governance arrangements. While it is often claimed that the reforms associated with NPM led to a hollowing out of the state as governments retreated from direct service delivery (Rhodes, 1996), others, like Skelcher (2000), argue instead that we saw an emergence of the 'congested state' with multiple different providers entering the field. The reality today is that there are ever-increasing numbers of organisations across different sectors collaborating in order to address 'wicked problems' (Head, 2014) – those issues that are generally considered so complex and problematic that they cannot be solved by the actions of one agency acting alone. They require collaborative responses to even understand what these issues are, how they are generated and where we might intervene to overcome these.

Of course, it would be misrepresenting history to argue that there was no plurality in the sources of public service provision prior to NPM (we need only remember primary care and residential care to refute that position). Nonetheless, successive UK governments came to realise that 'wicked problems' require (almost by definition) collaboration across agencies, and consequently the number of agencies that need to be involved in such collaboration increased. This pattern is not just confined to the UK and has been repeated across a range of other jurisdictions (Carey et al, 2016). The recent emphasis on collaborative working between health and social care is, therefore, in no small part, a consequence of the extensive influence of NPM.

'Steering' in health and social care has more recently come to mean commissioning in the English system, with Scotland, Wales and Northern Ireland taking different approaches that do not revolve in the same way around market-based mechanisms (Bevan et al, 2014). NHS and local authorities divesting themselves over time of provision – the rowing – has had two immediate results:

- First, collaboration must take place at – and between – two levels: commissioning organisations (for example, CCGs and local authorities) and providing organisations. No longer is the collaboration largely between two predominant hierarchical bureaucracies that combine responsibility both for strategic planning (*what*) and operational management (*how*), as was the case pre-1989 (albeit that neither CCGs nor local authorities are yet entirely free from aspects of direct provision).
- Second, integration has been pursued since 2000 in a policy environment that has encouraged contestability as much as

collaboration, which has left some managers and leaders – in particular in commissioning organisations – puzzling over the appropriate local balance in a context where the political messages over support for competition can be mixed (Field and Peck, 2003; Freeman and Peck, 2007).

In due course, it may be that even commissioning is seen as another form of rowing. The energetic expansion of direct payments and individual budgets has put significant amounts of commissioning responsibility and resources in the hands of private agencies and individual citizens (Needham, 2011). Alongside clinically led commissioning in primary care, this raises the question about what it is precisely that government agencies should focus on.

New public management to new public governance

In more recent years it has been argued that we are in the midst of a paradigm change, away from NPM and to new public governance (NPG) (Osborne, 2010). NPG provides a critique of what it sees as the negative impacts of NPM, and incorporates a commitment to policy networks and collaborative relationships between organisations and a focus on institutional relationships within society and government (Osborne, 2006, 2010). As an emerging theory and field of practice, NPG represents an attempt to capture how public administration currently operates and is executed by governments (and other policy actors) as it shifts away from hierarchical managerial practices. Having said this, many of the challenges of working across boundaries that characterise NPM remain areas of critical concern within NPG. NPG captures both problems left unresolved in NPM, as well as emerging issues associated with more networked forms of governance.

What is interesting about the NPG movement in terms of leadership and management is what it suggests is important in terms of skills and abilities of leaders and managers. In contrast to NPM with a focus on 'scientific management' and 'evidence-based policy and practice', NPG focuses on the kinds of softer skills that are needed to circumnavigate today's complex and hybrid terrain (Dickinson and Sullivan, 2014). Indeed, Rhodes (2014) has recently argued that traditional 'craft' skills of public managers are critical in an area of NPG, arguing 'I do not dispute that the public service needs new skills. But that it is a step too far to talk of these new skills as a "full blown cultural transformation"'. We return later to the issue of what skills are needed to lead and manage inter-agency collaboration in an effective way, but what we hoped to illustrate by way of this discussion is the complexity of the institutional context surrounding health and social care, and the range of different skills and abilities we therefore require leaders and managers to possess.

Collaboration and networks

In the context of health and social care, words such as collaboration, integration and partnership have often been used rather indiscriminately to refer to a range of ways of organising. For most of us it will come as no surprise that in everyday language similar sorts of terms are used to refer to different modes of organising. For example, many current health and social care 'partnerships' have become hierarchies. Equally, some market-based relationships – for example, public–private partnerships – are misleadingly described as 'partnerships', partly, perhaps, because they can involve long-term relationships, but mostly because use of this term may be politically more acceptable. These may not be entirely accurate descriptions of these words, but why should people be concerned with what are ultimately rather academic and theoretical terms? We argue that terminology is important, and its usage has important implications in terms of our understanding of a range of issues and thereby our interactions around these. In the remainder of this section we focus specifically on managing and leading in and around agencies attempting to collaborate within 'genuine' networks. What we mean by network in this context is 'a cross-sector, cross-organisational group, working together under some form of recognised governance, towards common goals which would be extremely difficult, if not impossible, to achieve if tackled by a single organisation' (Armistead et al, 2007, p 212).

There is a significant literature on networks, and it is helpful in aiding us to develop characteristics that are useful for those managing and leading in inter-agency settings. The good news is that this literature is enormous and the bad news is ... this literature is enormous. One attempt at classifying types of networks suggested by 6 et al (2006) is presented in a simplified form in Table 1.2. This typology suggests that there are at least seven distinct sets of drivers for the creation of networks. Of course these drivers may overlap in specific cases or, indeed, come into conflict (for example, when different motives are driving partners). Where drivers come into conflict it may be the case that not all these drivers can be successfully incorporated into any one composite network form (Kitchener, 2002, provides a wonderful illustration of this in describing a failed merger attempt during the creation of an Academic Health Science Center in the US).

The identification of these seven sets of drivers also suggests that the influence of individual or collective approaches to management and leadership may vary significantly between various forms of network (for example, this influence can be predicted to be much greater in personal networks than in those driven by technological innovations). In addition, it may be worth considering whether in any collaboration the espoused reasons for pursuing joint working (such as those in public consultation documents) tell the whole story of the drivers in play (Dickinson and Glasby, 2010; Dickinson, 2014). Many of these kinds of documents major on the drivers of *organisational competence* and/or *problem contingency*, when the timing and design of the network may be as much shaped by the financial and institutional context (that is, although it is often suggested that changes are an attempt to address certain issues, they may, in fact, also be driven by financial factors or due to other wider political or cultural pressures). It is also worth bearing in mind that prevailing political or organisational fashion may be a significant factor in the forms that local collaborations take (see, for example, Peck and 6, 2006).

6 et al (2006) suggest that another way of conceptualising networks is to link them to four basic ways of organising which are present in all organisations (see Figure 1.1). According to this framework, organisations can be classified according to the way that they

Table 1.2: A classification of types of networks

Theory	Driving force shaping networks	Distinct form of networks based on
Resource exchange/financial (in particular reducing transaction costs)	Focus on securing and optimising efficient use of resources (and minimisation of transaction costs)	*Content*, that is, the nature of the resources – money, staff – exchanged
Organisational competence and learning	Focus on securing new competencies and knowledge (and maximisation of benefits)	*Content*, that is the competencies and knowledge desired
Personal	Focus on connections between individuals (and thus organisations)	*Structure*, or the overall pattern formed by these personal connections
Institutional	Focus on patterns of established authority, accountability and procedures in organisations joining network	*Institution*, with each example shaped by the local interaction of these patterns
Ecological	Focus on organisational interests in forming clusters to exploit specific resources in particular niches	*Content*, that is, the nature of the niche to be exploited
Problem/technology contingency	Focus on solving particular problems	*Institution*, with each example shaped by the nature of the problem and the potential solution
Macro-economic/technological determinist	Focus on the consequences of technology available to solve problems	*Content*, with each example shaped by the nature of and innovations in technology

Source: Adapted from 6 et al (2006)

predominantly organise themselves; as a consequence, there is a form of network that they will favour. These four forms differ from each other in terms of the sorts of behaviours and styles of sense-making that are important (Chapter 3 explores the issue of sense-making in more detail).

Figure 1.1: Conceptualising networks around four basic ways of organising

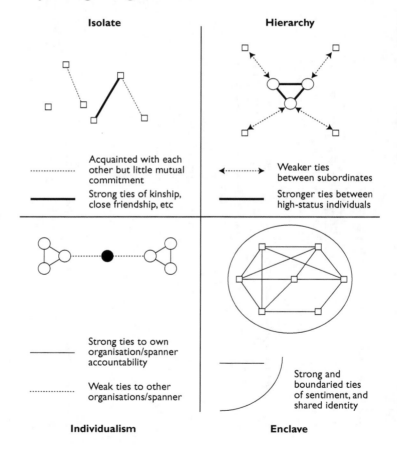

Isolate

.... Acquainted with each other but little mutual commitment

———— Strong ties of kinship, close friendship, etc

Hierarchy

◄·········► Weaker ties between subordinates

———— Stronger ties between high-status individuals

———— Strong ties to own organisation/spanner accountability

.... Weak ties to other organisations/spanner

———— Strong and boundaried ties of sentiment, and shared identity

Individualism

Enclave

In reality, individual organisations exhibit a combination of – also known as a 'settlement between' – these ways of organising. When agencies work collaboratively with other organisations, each individual partner is obliged to seek a compromise between its preferred way of organising and those of its partners. At this stage, it is important to note that this theory suggests that by determining the characteristics of collaborations in terms of these ways of organising, managers and leaders may be able to behave in ways that are more harmonious with the prevailing settlement (Box 1.3 clarifies this with examples). In other words, if leaders and managers can act in ways that are consistent with the form of settlement, then they may find that their actions are more acceptable and accepted by individuals and organisations (and this is congruent with ideas articulated in situational theories of leadership outlined below).

Box 1.3: Network forms and management styles

- A manager in a *hierarchical network* will have authority derived from their position and will achieve impact by calling on the formal rules and roles of the partnership.
- A manager in an *enclave network* will get their authority from commitment to the cause and achieve impact by appealing to the shared goals of the partnership.
- A manager in an *individualistic network* will get their authority by an ability to connect disparate organisations and individuals and achieve impact by the outputs and outcomes that these alignments can deliver.
- A manager in an *isolate network* – something of a contradiction in terms – will struggle to gain authority or achieve impact but may do so through the power of personal relationships.

It is important to note that most networks will actually be hybrids that combine elements of all of these four ways of organising, and managers will need to be able to judge the most appropriate interventions for the hybrid in which they are operating.

Theories of management and leadership

So far this discussion has introduced some of the complexities related to notions of health and social care collaboration and clarified some of the characteristics that may help describe the specific challenges of, and approaches to, managing within them. The remainder of this chapter explores some of the current major ideas around management and leadership. Unfortunately, these theories are as complex in nature as the issues surrounding collaboration. In seeking clarity about the nature of management and leadership in inter-agency settings, the definition offered by O'Leary et al (2006) of collaborative public management may be helpful. They argue that it is '[A] concept that describes the process of facilitating and operating in multi-organisational arrangements to solve problems that cannot be solved or easily solved by single organisations. Collaborative means co-labour, to cooperate to achieve common goals, working across boundaries in multisector relationships' (p 7).

To date, we have used management and leadership interchangeably; however, much of the literature proclaims that there is a clear distinction to be made. Where leaders are transformational, managers are transactional (Zaleznik, 1992; Dubrin, 2004). The former do the right thing, while the latter merely do the thing right (Bennis, 1994). A helpful distinction for our present purposes is articulated by Grint (2005b), who argues that the distinction between management and leadership is best understood through an analysis of the problem to be solved (wicked, tame or critical), and the nature of the power to be exercised (hard power or soft power) (see Figure 1.2). In his framework:

- *Critical problems* require an immediate intervention with hard power and therefore demand a command response (where the priority is to provide an answer).
- *Tame problems* are ones that organisations have seen before and thus have an established reaction, and require a managerial response (where the priority is to organise a process).

Figure 1.2: A typology of problems, power and authority

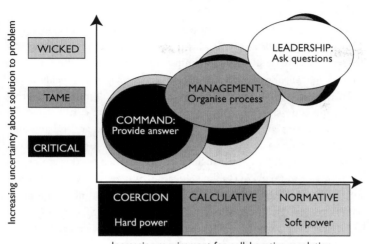

Source: Adapted from Grint (2005a, p 1477)

- *Wicked problems* are the sort that health and social care collaborations are typically established to address, and require a leadership response that deploys soft power (where the priority is to ask questions).

There is potential compatibility between transaction and organising processes, and transformation and asking questions (with critical problems relating to a command mode of leadership or management). Nonetheless, Grint is careful not to make extravagant claims on behalf of leaders (and he has a very particular perspective on the role of leaders in posing these questions, to which we shall come back shortly). As an example of the use of this framework, Dickinson et al (2011) employ Grint's taxonomy in exploring the kinds of activities that leaders of priority setting processes face in health and social care. From their analysis of the different roles that leaders and managers play, they conclude that the most important activities relate not to the technical components of these processes (difficult as they are), but to influencing those over which they have few hard levers of power.

In contrast to those who would make a firm distinction between leadership and management, Pye (2005, p 35) suggests that 'it seems much less significant when what really matters is (effective) organising.' This seems to us both an insightful and pragmatic observation. As a consequence, we will use leadership from here on to represent *those activities that might enable effective organising, especially within collaborations*.

Turning now to the more conceptual literature, despite the fact that leadership is possibly one of the most researched topics of the past 50 years, it remains a contested topic, under-theorised and reliant on a few popular views and perspectives (Bolden and Gosling, 2006). Van Wart (2003, p 225) argues that the lack of evidence for this concept is even greater in terms of public leadership, where 'the needs are great and the research opportunities are manifold.' Alvesson and Sveningsson (2003) suggest that the lack of a universal definition of leadership may be helpful; they argue that a single definition is not practically possible (given the range of different ways that the term has been employed), and even if it was, it might hinder the growth of new ways of thinking about leadership that do not conform to the established definition. As we have already illustrated in this chapter, there are a broad number of different mechanisms used to drive collaboration within contemporary health and social care contexts, and it likely therefore that we need many different definitions of what leadership is contingent on the specific locale it is being operated within.

In the first edition of this book we noted the relatively sparse amount of literature that directly considers management and leadership within collaborative settings. Despite vast tracts being written on the topics of both collaboration and leadership since this time, this observation still holds today (Chapman et al, 2015; Vogel and Masal, 2015). Against this background we briefly explore the wider management and leadership literature to illuminate some of the key theories and perspectives surrounding leadership, and also consider the different skills and competencies which leadership in collaborative settings may require in comparison to more 'traditional' models. Drawing on Peck and Dickinson (2009), we identify six broad models of leadership that, while they have emerged mostly sequentially, still remain influential in

Table 1.3: Summary of major approaches to leadership

Approach	Emphasis	Development implications
Great man	Personal traits	Few – leaders are born, not made
Situational/personal–situational	Context dependence	Can develop the interpersonal to some degree, but mostly developing use of different approaches in certain contexts
Psychological profiling	Psychological traits	Limited development of the interpersonal
Behavioural	Actions appropriate to followership	Development of the intrapersonal
Transformational	Relationship between leader and followers	Development of the inter and intrapersonal
Post-transformational	Sense-making	Development of the inter and intrapersonal

the literature today. These are summarised, along with their implications for leadership development interventions, in Table 1.3. As this table clearly demonstrates, the kinds of skills needed, the approaches used to develop leadership and whether we believe leadership can be developed at all, depend on the kind of approach that we believe is in place at any given time.

Much of the early literature focused on the leadership of 'great men'. Such approaches regard the innate characteristics of the individual as imperative, with context having little influence. According to this perspective, leaders are born. Although certain aspects of leaders may be developed through training programmes, it is unlikely that someone who is not born with these 'great man' traits will be able to be developed into a leader. The remnants of trait theory can be seen in accounts of both transformational leaders (for example, charisma) and boundary spanners (for example, creativity). In health and social care settings, the 'great man' approach seems alive and kicking (Martin and Learmonth, 2009). As Ford et al (2008) observe, narratives around heroism and masculinity are certainly still firmly embedded within our expectations of healthcare leaders.

In contrast to trait theorists, the *situational* approach suggests that leadership styles have to be adopted as a response to the demands of a given situation; contextual factors thus determine who emerges as a leader. In time, this led to the evolution of *personal–situational* theories. These maintain that, in any given case of leadership, some aspects are due to the situation, some result from the person and yet others are consequent on the combination of the two (Bass, 1960). This way of thinking established that there was a crucial relationship between context and leadership that was to prove increasingly influential and, indeed, still shapes many leadership development programmes delivered today.

After the Second World War, writers developed notions of leadership based on a number of factors which, again, put the individual centre stage: the interrelations between individuals (Likert, 1961); individual motivation (Maslow, 1954); the interdependence between individuals and organisations (Blake and Moulton, 1965); and the fit between individual and organisational needs (McGregor, 1966). These writers established the importance of the individual's *psychological profile* to leadership, representing in some ways the return of a more sophisticated form of trait theory. Perhaps the best-known psychological inventory – the Myers Briggs Type Inventory – was initially put together by psychologists in the 1940s (Briggs Myers, 2000), and is still widely used in leadership development programmes. These writers also set the stage for the entrance of concepts that are also now commonplace, for example, 'emotional intelligence' (that is, an ability to perceive, assess or manage the emotions of an individual's self and of others) (Salovey and Mayer, 1990; Goleman, 1996). George (2000) stresses the importance of four aspects of emotional intelligence to leadership: the appraisal and expression of emotion, the use of emotion to enhance decision-making, knowledge about emotions and the management of emotions. These theorists, with their stress on the importance of the personal resources of the individual, found their ideas very much back in favour when the solutions to the problems of late 20th-century corporations were seen as lying in the capabilities of chief executives (Storey, 2004a).

During roughly the same period, a number of accounts took further the idea that the interaction between the person and the situation was of paramount importance, and also started to raise the profile of followers. *Path-goal theory* (House, 1971) suggested that successful leaders show their follower the rewards that are available and the paths (that is, the behaviours) through which these rewards may be obtained (and this seems to have resonance with the approach adopted towards health and social care by the Department of Health three decades later, in the notion of 'earned autonomy' as associated with NHS foundation trusts). *Contingency theory* (Fiedler, 1967) argued, rather simplistically, that leaders have a tendency towards either task-orientation or relation-oriented leadership (that is, leaders either focus on tasks or on relationships). Later, Vroom and colleagues (Vroom and Yetton, 1973; Vroom and Jago, 1988) elaborated this theory by postulating that three factors influence the choice of leadership style:

- degree of structuring of the problem
- amount of information available
- quality of decision required.

Hersey and Blanchard (1988) added as an additional variable the readiness of followers to accept leadership. While sharing the limitations of other theories in this tradition – for example, paying no regard to the constraints imposed on leaders by the pre-existing patterns of authority, accountability and procedures within organisations (Giddens, 1993) – the suggestion that leaders can identify (and indeed, in the argument of Grint, 2005a, operationalise) factors that might influence their selection of leadership style has become important.

Before *transformational leadership* made its entrance on to the theoretical stage in the 1990s, it was preceded by charismatic leadership. In many respects, this signalled a return to the certainties of the 'great man' era. Perhaps best seen as one, and only one, characteristic of transformational leaders – a necessary but not a sufficient condition – the charisma of chief executives was a cause for celebration in the 1980s (see, for example, Peters and Waterman, 1982) and a cause for concern

20 years later (Mangham, 2004). Perhaps the most considered overview of this theory is provided by Bryman (1992). Although many writers (for example, Bass, 1990) have given sober accounts of the attributes of transformational leaders towards their followers – for example, individualised consideration, intellectual stimulation, inspirational motivation and idealised influence (that is, providing a role model) – others can look aspirational and, on occasions, fanciful (see, for example, Alimo-Metcalfe, 1998; Boje and Dennehey, 1999, respectively). Nonetheless, the transformational trope can draw attention to two often overlooked aspects of leadership (both of which are highlighted by Grint, 2005b). First, the identity of a leader – charismatic or otherwise – is relational rather than individual. That is, 'leadership is a function of a community not a result derived from an individual deemed to be objectively superhuman' (Grint, 2005b, p 2). Second, leadership has to be embodied: 'leadership is essentially hybrid in nature – it comprises humans, clothes, adornments, technologies, cultures, rules and so on' (Grint, 2005b, p 2); that is, it has to be performed. This latter dimension of leadership is becoming increasingly important and is the subject of a separate section in Chapter 3.

Finally, there are also signs of some new trends emerging; these seem to suggest a number of directions that have not yet coalesced into a 'school' (which is presumably why Storey, 2004b, gives them the name 'post-transformational'). The most important of these focuses on leadership as sense-making (see Chapter 3 for more on this concept). Fullan (2001) draws on the seminal work of Weick (for example, 1995) who provides an accessible introduction to the notion of sense-making: 'Active agents construct ... events. They "structure the unknown".... How they construct what they construct, why, and with what effects are the central questions for people interested in sensemaking' (p 4). As Weick puts it, 'sensemaking is about authoring as well as reading' (p 7); for him, it involves creation as much as discovery. The importance of Weick's work here is that it emphasises the potential for changing the way in which organisational pasts, presents and futures are constructed by organisational members and, in particular, by the interventions of organisational leaders.

Fullan (2001) identifies five independent but mutually reinforcing components of effective leadership:

- moral purpose
- understanding the change process
- relationship building
- knowledge creation and sharing
- coherence making.

The focus on this last element – leaders as sense-makers – is central to papers on leadership by Grint (for example, 2005a) and Peck and Dickinson (2009) – where the purpose of leaders asking questions is to enable consensual construction of the nature of the problem. There is also a range of theories that can broadly be described as theorising 'distributed leadership' that, it is argued, may be particularly relevant to collaboration and is covered in more detail in Chapter 3. These include ideas around informal leaders (Hosking, 1988), decentred leadership (Martin, 1992), shared leadership (Judge and Ryman, 2001) and other forms of distributed or plural leadership. While these accounts are not always entirely clear about what is being distributed (and by whom) – or whether it is being actively distributed or merely taken – they do acknowledge the organisational reality of the power of what elsewhere have been termed 'street-level bureaucrats' (Lipsky, 1980). This refers to the ability of front-line professionals to organise local procedures and practices to suit their own interests (although the date of Lipsky's study suggests that this tendency may not be especially limited to collaborative arrangements).

Structure and agency

The final issue that we reflect on in this opening chapter is the relationship between structure and agency. These two concepts are important within the social theory literature in explaining what influences activity in any given setting. The idea of structure refers to the sorts of formalised characteristics that typify given contexts such as the statutory context, the financial and resource framework being operated within, performance management frameworks, social, environmental and economic drivers and so on. Agency, meanwhile, refers to the ability of individuals to consciously act in order to reach a set of individual intentions (Hay, 1995). As Sullivan et al (2012, p 56) describe, 'Agency is the ability to set and pursue one's own goals and interests, which may be individual or societal. Agency focuses attention on action, what motivates it, what influences the choice of action and what constrains or confines it.' It is important for us to draw your attention to these concepts at this point as different parts of the literature often focus more on one of these factors than the other.

Williams (2012, p 23) observes that 'a defining characteristic of the literature on collaboration is that it favours an organisational and institutional focus at the expense of micro-level examination.' As we see in the discussion of the leadership and management literature set out above, arguably this has often been far more concerned with the individuals who occupy leadership roles than the structural context. Meanwhile, the collaboration literature has focused on structures, organisations and institutions at the expense of individual actors, while the leadership literature has often focused on individuals at the expense of their interaction with followers and organisations, institutions and structures. Sullivan et al (2012) argue that a more fruitful way to think about collaborative leadership is in terms of situated agency, where individuals are influenced but not determined by structures, and internal understandings and frameworks are as important as external actions. In research with Welsh public managers, Sullivan and colleagues find that structure and agency are important in the shaping of leadership outcomes, approaches and behaviours, and that these factors come together in dynamic ways. In practice what this means is that it is difficult to provide one framework that will work for leading and managing in inter-agency settings as each activity is influenced by a range of different factors. What this means in practice is that managers and leaders must pay close attention to the values, beliefs and ideas present in any given context, and focus on managing the tensions and conflicts between these. It also explains why we might find very different outcomes from contexts that from an outsider perspective look rather similar. The relationship between structure and agency is one we will return to on a number of occasions in this book, and we will elaborate on these concepts further with practical examples of their meaning.

In this chapter we have provided much food for thought on the subjects of collaboration, leadership and the relationship between them. However, most of this material has been prescriptive (saying how things ought to be) rather than analytical (reflecting on research undertaken in the field). In the next chapter we move on to the research literature, and explore what the limited evidence tells us about how we might lead and manage different forms of collaborative relationships.

Reflective exercises

1. Think of a person who represents an effective leader to you. This may be someone you know or else someone from the media, politics, sport or other domains. What is it about this individual that makes you believe them to be an effective leader?

2. Of the different approaches to leadership in Table 1.3, which are you familiar with and do you recognise within your organisation and others that you work with? Do these different approaches seem to deliver different results?

3. Think of an individual you have encountered in your professional or private life who you would describe as a boundary spanner. Why is it you believe them to be a boundary spanner? What skills or attributes does this individual possess which you think makes them suitable for this role?

4. In what ways do you think that the leadership and management of collaboration are similar or different to these activities in 'traditional' organisational settings?

5. Identify a list of the major challenges facing your organisation. Are these critical, tame or wicked issues? What mode of leadership or management is currently being used to address these issues? Is this appropriate? How might it be improved?

Further reading and resources

- For an overview of leadership theory, see Peck and Dickinson's (2009) *Performing leadership*.
- For an overview of the literature on boundary spanners, Williams' (2012) *Collaboration in public policy and practice* provides an accessible and comprehensive introduction.
- Useful websites for leaders and managers include:
  - NHS Leadership Academy: www.leadershipacademy.nhs.uk/
  - British Academy of Management: www.bam.ac.uk
  - Centre for Workplace Leadership (Australia): www.workplaceleadership.com.au/
  - Social Leadership Australia: http://leadership.benevolent.org.au/
  - Chartered Management Institute: www.managers.org.uk
  - Centre for Social Impact, Leadership framework: www.csi.edu.au/about-social/social-impact-framework/leadership/
  - The Ready to Manage website hosts an annual rating on the best leadership blog each year, and the 2015 rankings can be found at the following link, along with a sense of what these different blogs offer: http://blog.readytomanage.com/best-50-leadership-blog-sites-in-2015/

2

What does research tell us?

In this chapter we explore the research evidence in order to better understand precisely what it is that we know about leading and managing in inter-agency settings. We explore different network forms and their characteristics, difficulties and outcomes, the attributes of collaborative leaders, and consider the life cycle of collaborations and the implications of this for management and leadership. As we have previously argued, leadership is currently a concept in vogue, and we must be cautious not to imbue leadership with ambitions that are simply unrealistic. We shall return in Chapter 3 to the idea of leadership as performance – and the limitations within this – but at this stage it is sufficient to note that at least part of the trajectory followed by any collaborative arrangement will be determined by the patterns of authority, accountability and procedure that carry weight in the agencies that join and the interaction between them (this is the institutional element contained in Table 1.2). Before moving on to the attributes of leaders, we explore the evidence for leadership and the degree to which it has been demonstrated to deliver improved performance.

Is leadership 'the answer'?

The idea of leadership is centrally embedded within Western culture and is often viewed as a crucial factor in the effective functioning of many aspects of society. The public sector is no different, with Lambright and Quinn (2011, p 782) arguing that 'nothing in public administration is more important, interesting, or mysterious than leadership.' Given this observation it is perhaps of little surprise that in the investigation into what went wrong with the terrible abuses of care at Stafford Hospital that Robert Francis should highlight a failure of leadership as being a key issue. Francis (2013) found that leadership at Mid Staffordshire was 'significantly lacking' with the trust board being inexperienced and over-confident. In the government's response (Secretary of State for Health, 2013), they highlighted the development of 'excellence in leadership' as being a key task in preventing such issues from recurring, and in recent years significant numbers of individuals have completed the NHS Leadership Academy's programmes, which aim to equip people appropriately for a range of leadership roles.

Within the context of collaborative working, leadership has often been viewed as an important way in which different partners can be brought together. At a local level, therefore, leadership can be assumed to be responsible for part of the way in which collaborations develop. Where collaborative endeavours have failed to produce the intended results, a number of studies have suggested that the problem is a lack of leadership (see, for example, Mitchell and Shortell, 2000; Weiss et al, 2002; Rugkåsa et al, 2007). Thus, leadership is often identified retrospectively as being a key factor in the success or otherwise of collaborative arrangements. In the case of personalistic networks (again, see Table 1.2), where the interactions of organisations are regarded as the consequence of relationships between individuals, the space for management and leadership to exert influence may be presumed to be at its most potent. However, it is our view that this personal element should be seen as representing one of the potential facets of leadership – the *networker* showing *relational competence*, for instance – rather than as a distinct form of network in its own right. This is on the basis that any network purely rooted in individual contacts that did not connect with the broader aspirations of the organisations concerned – such as the need to pursue *problem sharing and problem solving* – would only either serve the interests of the individuals concerned and/or be short-lived (and there is evidence for studies of Health Action Zones; see Barnes et al, 2005).

Perhaps again, therefore, we should be a little cautious here about the enthusiasm of some research for the leader as key variable in leadership success. Ford et al (2008, p 11) go as far as to argue that leadership is an 'empty signifier'; in other words, it is something that cannot be realised: leadership is 'an object whose existence is impossible but which is central to that discourse of which it is a part.' With these observations in mind, perhaps the question should not be 'did leadership lead to the success of this collaboration?' but 'how big a part does leadership really play in the trajectory of effective collaboration?' Pollitt (2000) notes that within the history of the NHS there is something of an uncritical acceptance and implementation of the latest simple prescription for improvement; in recent years, this has undoubtedly included transformational leadership (see, for example, Bevan, 2005) and more recently, distributed or collective leadership (West et al, 2014). In respect to this latter model of leadership, Martin and Learmonth (2012, p 281) note 'how leadership is increasingly conferred not only on those in positions of formal power but on frontline clinicians, patients and even the public, and how not just the implementation but the design of policy is now constructed as being led by these groups. Such constructions of the distribution of power in the health service, however, contradict the picture drawn by academic work.' This quote demonstrates what Lawler (2004) outlines as the assumption that leadership is desirable, that people will welcome it and that it is necessarily unequivocally a 'good thing'. As a consequence, it is frequently identified as a crucial factor within the literature for organisations seeking high performance. This reinforces Gemmill and Oakley's (1992) argument that leadership might, in fact, be a 'social fiction'; that is, because leadership is increasingly seen as unquestionably crucial to effective organisations, one of the causal factors of effective organisations must be leadership.

As a consequence of leadership currently being so in vogue, commentators may tend to attribute a number of changes or outcomes to leadership when they may, in fact, have been influenced by other factors. Jim Collins (2001) suggests that this reflects a tendency to view 'leadership as the answer to everything'. This has the potential to severely limit progress; in our enthusiasm for leadership we may well be overlooking other important causal factors when considering the success (or, indeed, failure) of collaborative endeavours.

Finally, we cannot simply presume that leadership always has positive impacts (see Mangham, 2004; Lauchs et al, 2011). O'Toole and Meier (2004) investigate what they call the 'dark side' of network management, and suggest that there are some potentially negative impacts that might flow from these processes (particularly relating to benefits accruing around certain groups and not others); it may be that Vangen and Huxham (2003) are referring to such consequences arising from the 'collaborative thuggery' that we discuss below.

What does the evidence say about managing and leading collaboration?

As we have previously noted, the literature relating to leading (and managing) in inter-agency settings is limited in terms of scope, focus and consistency. In a review of the evidence on public leadership, Vogel and Masal (2015) found that this literature predominantly focuses on functional approaches to leadership (that is, analysing the impact of leadership on dependent variables such as services performance), with only a small number of papers studying collaborative leadership. Even where studies do deal with this topic, it is primarily in terms of *describing* shifts in leadership practices in moving from hierarchy to network modes of governance, but not establishing a significant evidence base in relation to this topic – either in terms of outcomes or the practice of leadership. Despite this, much of the collaboration literature still makes bold claims about the role of leaders in managing sets of complex organisational, structural and cultural factors. With the lessons about overstating claims for leadership set out above in mind, we now move to question the extent to which claims about leadership in collaborative settings are evidence-based. For example, many of the claims made for boundary-spanning roles pertain to transformational models of leaders as charismatic individuals; is there robust evidence for the efficacy of this style or, in practice, does inter-agency leadership relate more to shared *leadership* than to traditional models of the individual *leader*? This is a question to which we shall return.

When inter-agency leadership is featured in research, it is frequently presented in contrast to that within 'traditional' organisations (see, for example, Sullivan and Skelcher, 2002; McCallin, 2003; Goldsmith and Eggers, 2004). Table 2.1 represents one such example of the genre. While not unhelpful, it does seem a little naive in its presentation of the 'classical' perspective. As argued in the previous chapter, in our experience of health and social care, many of the challenges within single organisations require the 'network' perspective; in some ways such approaches merely serve to present the over-simplistic transactional/transformational dichotomy in a new guise.

Table 2.1: 'Classical' and network management compared

Perspective dimensions	'Classical' perspective	Network perspective
Organisational setting	Single authority structure	Divided authority structure
Goal structure	Activities are guided by clear goals and well-defined problems	Various and challenging definitions of problems and goals
Role of manager	System controller	Mediator, process manager, network builder
Management tasks	Planning and guiding organisational processes	Guiding interactions and providing opportunities
Management activities	Planning, designing, leading	Guiding interactions and providing opportunities

Source: Adapted from Kickert et al (1997)

In the course of the following discussion we summarise the research literature that relates specifically to networks, given that these forms are often argued to demand rather different approaches of leaders than traditional approaches. First, we consider the implications for leadership of different forms of collaborative endeavours. Subsequently, we explore evidence on what leaders are thought to bring to inter-agency settings and the roles that research suggests they actually achieve – or the issues they have the ability to influence – in practice.

Different network forms: their characteristics, difficulties and outcomes

The discussion of forms of networks presented here draws in part on the work of 6 et al (2006). Overall, they note, the general findings of Bass' (1974) review of the leadership literature are no doubt relevant to interorganisational contexts. That is, effective leaders need to achieve network centrality, establish areas of influence and span structural 'holes' regardless of the particular form of the network. However, as noted in Chapter 1, one fruitful way to think about leadership is to look at the structural position of leaders in their personal networks. That is, to consider their role within organisational networks, the ways in which they interact with other individuals or organisations as well as their organisational structure or context. The networked perspective suggests that we should look at leaders in the present context as 'boundary spanners', which is very much the position taken by Williams (2012) in his study of boundary spanners.

Resource exchange networks

Thompson (1967) presented a model of the organisation as consisting of a core of activities, the boundaries of which are buffered by certain functions which protect the integrity of the core, but are also spanned by certain categories of role holders charged with bringing in certain resources (or taking them out). This is predominantly a *resource exchange* model (many studies privilege this approach as economists have been very active in the network literature). These roles may be involved in both shielding the core from external threats and in bridging to external opportunities. Overall, what distinguishes *resource exchange networks* is that, as 6 et al (2006, p 16) summarise, they can be defensive – 'inter-organisational forms are driven by factors that are predominantly negative, that is by the pressure to reduce such costs and by the imperative to avoid failures in transactions' – or more positive – 'based around the tendency of individuals or organisations to pursue both competitive and comparative advantage and therefore market power. They do so by configuring their tangible and intangible assets, skills, resources and relationships in order to optimise their benefits' (p 16). Note that, in both cases, the organisational motivations are essentially self-interested.

Thompson (1967) also distinguished between cases in which the boundary-spanning function worked to highly prescribed rules on transactions with external organisations (*predictability*) and those where the boundary spanners have discretion (*entrepreneur*). Examples from commercial organisations which stress *predictability* – and are thus perhaps more defensive in orientation – would include account managers who are responsible for managing downstream vertical ties with customers and purchasing and procurement managers charged with handling upstream vertical ties along the supply chain (Katz and Kahn, 1966). There are also accounts of boundary spanners who are more *entrepreneurial*, responsible for horizontal network maintenance, because they are charged with liaising with particular interorganisational groups, representing the organisation externally, or forming coalitions (see Aldrich and Herker, 1977); this clearly is the more positive mode. In the latter case, we are also moving towards the *ecological* perspective on networks to which we turn shortly. Box 2.1 presents an example of a resource exchange network.

Box 2.1: Beyond the Bell, Great South Coast, Australia

The Beyond the Bell project aims to improve young people's chances of attaining Year 12 or equivalent, and better prepare them for a successful transition to the next phase of their lives. A 'collective impact' approach has been taken where the 'project working group recognises that no single person, organisation or sector, however innovative or powerful can accomplish the projects goals alone.' The approach is a structured way of bringing collaborators together to work together, requiring them to move from traditional isolated impact approaches, and can lead to large-scale, long-term and systematic change. Beyond the Bell aims to overcome a history of competition for resources between local governments, organisations and other agencies. The initiative has a regional leadership group, in an effort to reduce this competition, and local action groups embedded in each local government that are charged with implementation. Despite this, challenges naturally remain. Over the last three years, Beyond the Bell has found the following strategies to be helpful:

- presenting to meetings as individuals, leaving behind organisational allegiances and other agendas;
- a generosity of spirit, humility, courage and ability to listen deeply (suspending personal views);
- not everything needs to come to the group 'for approval';
- letting go of 'being the expert' and wanting to be in control;
- disagreements should be shared openly, rather than behind-the-scenes lobbying to support particular positions;
- scheduling time for reflection and learning as part of the meeting agenda.

Source: Collaboration for Impact (www.collaborationforimpact.com/leadership-at-beyond-the-bell-great-south-coast-vic/)

Problem-sharing and problem-solving networks

As we have already argued, many health and social care collaborative endeavours aim to tackle the perceived 'wicked' issues that face society. In terms of the implications of these for network forms, as 6 et al (2006, pp 18-19) argue,

> ... the structures and capabilities of different forms of inter-organisational relations are shaped most by the prevailing technologies of production that require (or do not require) particular inter-organisational links with other organisations possessing access to other specific technologies. The argument suggests that once the nature of the task and the nature of the technologies necessary for undertaking that task have been established, then the structure, form of accountability

and efficacy of the network forms that will most suit those conditions can, at least in principle, be identified.

Problem-sharing and problem-solving networks have been extensively researched through the example of Health Action Zones, area-based initiatives that sought multiagency bids from health and local authorities to address specific local problems (Barnes et al, 2005). As 6 et al (2006) also note, the assumed fit between the nature of the problems and the choice of the partnership form to address them is not typically borne out in experience. Boxes 2.2 and 2.3 present examples of *problem-sharing and problem-solving* collaborations, and the lessons about leadership and management that they suggest.

One further point that it is important to raise about problem-sharing and problem-solving networks relates to the nature of problems. Anyone who has ever studied policy will be well aware that problems exist in the eye of the beholder – in other words, what constitutes a problem for one person may not necessarily for another (Smith, 2014). This can pose a challenge for these forms of networks. As Peck et al (2002, p 40) concluded in their study of what is often considered to be the first major health and social care collaboration in Somerset, 'the establishment of the combined Trust did not – at the conclusion of the evaluation period – appear to have delivered significant benefits that have not been delivered elsewhere in England without the transfer of social care staff to NHS employment.' In other words, the adoption of the specific integrative approach was not essential to the sharing and solving of the problem (in this case, enhanced professional coordination in service delivery). Second, the problem shared and solved between the hierarchies of the NHS and local authority had no impact on the problems perceived by the clients of the service as priorities that, after three years of merger, were as pressing as ever. This suggests that *customer focus*, while important in the prescriptions for attributes of network leaders, may not appear very strongly in the empirical literature.

Box 2.2: Action Zones

One of the most significant innovations in government-sponsored partnership working was the creation of Action Zones (covering health, education and employment) during New Labour's first term (for an overview, see Powell and Moon, 2001). Promising additional resources and some non-specific relaxation of rules of engagement, localities were awarded 'Zone' status following a competitive process.

Interestingly, the extensive national evaluation of Health Action Zones re-confirms many of the challenges identified earlier, and adds some new ones (for example, the problems of engaging voluntary and community groups; see Matka et al, 2002), and says little about the nature of leadership in these collaborations.

In the final report on the development of collaborative capacity (Barnes et al, 2004, p 63), the researchers do note, however, that: 'the pressures and conflicting priorities sometimes faced by "middle managers" need to be acknowledged, and these players need to be empowered to act in ways that will enhance collaboration rather than otherwise.' This suggests that the most intractable organisational obstacles that collaborative leaders may face do not lie in either senior executives or front-line professionals; they argue that it is in the middle manager tier that 'the tension between innovation and meeting performance targets can be acute' (p 64). They also observe that committed individuals are crucial, and agencies need to invest in the development of such capacity. More recent literature has continued to stress the importance of middle management in influencing both up and down in the implementation process (Ahearne et al, 2014).

Box 2.3: Local strategic partnerships

The national evaluation of local strategic partnerships (LSPs), an initiative that developed further the aspirations that underpinned Action Zones, contained a specific paper on leadership issues (ODPM, 2005b), and a number of studies since (see, for example, Russell et al, 2010) have highlighted the importance of effective leadership for the success of these mechanisms. These nationally prescribed arrangements, initially established to respond to share and solve overall problems defined by government that were reflected in a significant list of centrally imposed targets, bring together health, the local authority and the wider community of public, voluntary and commercial agencies (Dickinson, 2014).

The national evaluation identified three stages to partnership – dialogue, strategy formation and delivery – and three parallel fields of leadership – political leadership, which supplies democratic legitimacy and the resources and power of the local authority; leadership from partner organisations; and leadership within the community (see Rugkåsa et al, 2007, for an account of boundary spanners working 'downwards'), which means securing the consent and active engagement of the wider community.

It may be that in seeking for unique features of leading in collaborations that this idea of boundary spanners working simultaneously across three apparently distinct ways of organising may be useful.

Learning networks

Of course, *learning* is also a key driver of large public sector collaboration. On this account, 6 et al (2006, p 17) argue that:

> ... agencies are presumed to make astute and intelligent judgements of the competence requirements of their field, the links they will seek to form with other firms will be ones that enable them to enhance their own core competencies. Such

links will seek to generate efficient and effective divisions of labour between partners in order to secure the competencies and capabilities that the firms do not have the ability, need or wish to cultivate internally.

In a study of regeneration partnerships, Hemphill et al (2006, p 75) found that 'one of the recurring responses centred on the collective learning and associated benefits that the members felt they gained from being part of a multisector partnership.' Davies (2004) suggests that a habit of collaborative working can be generated which fosters an almost ideological commitment to collaboration, which then results in more joint activity. This is an interesting suggestion that *learning* can apply to the process of doing collaboration – and lead to a tendency to see more of it as the solution to all sorts of challenges – and not just the content of the original collaboration.

The literature suggests that, although information-sharing networks are often best driven by their members (see 6 et al, 2006), this does not necessarily make them easy to maintain. Sermeus et al (2001) examine the network of hospitals known as the Belgian-Dutch Clinical Pathway Network, where membership had to be sustained by continuous efforts in persuasion. Similarly, a study on Project CHAIN (Community Health Alliances through Integrated Networks), a university-supported information network around improving the quality of life for older people in South Wales (Warner et al, 2003), suggests that, without mandatory membership and lacking any well pre-defined output, even developing protocols for coordination in community-based medication required extensive work to stabilise the membership and negotiate with powerful and sometimes mutually suspicious professions (and these studies suggest that *commitment* may well be a key characteristic of some effective network leaders).

In many countries managed clinical networks have been established to bring together professionals from a range of different teams and organisations in a context in which the delivery of care services is becoming ever more specialist (Thomas, 2003). Managed clinical networks have been viewed as one way of overcoming issues of fragmentation and sharing learning around a particular topic. Depending on the problem being addressed, this might include primary, secondary or tertiary care across different geographical areas. They can cover a particular disease or specialty or function or location. However, one of the observations made in a study of different clinical networks by Addicott et al (2007) is that if the broader context is not conducive to the operation of the network, then it will not be successful. If they are simply seen as a structural panacea and something that is quite simply just adopted in each locality, they are unlikely to succeed. Networks take time and attention and need professionals to engage with and to drive these processes (Ferlie et al, 2011). In their study of Australian clinical networks, Haines et al (2012, p 7) conclude, 'there is an urgent need to understand the factors that increase the likelihood that clinical networks will be effective because they are being widely implemented in Australia and other countries.' From the literature there is often a sense that clinical networks have focused more on *problem solving and problem sharing* than necessarily on *learning*. Box 2.4 sets out an example of an initiative that has been established specifically for learning in the context of collaborative working.

Box 2.4: Power to Persuade initiative

The Australian-run Power to Persuade (PTP) initiative is an example of a learning and connecting network. It was founded in 2012 to help develop these networks across different sectors, including government, community, private and academic. The key objectives are to contribute to assist in the creation of open and informal policy networks through addressing current skill and knowledge gaps, and to connect new and existing actors to knowledge and resources needed to improve policy development. The initiative does this by providing new spaces (both virtual and in person) for individuals to come together and 'meet differently', that is, in a way that considers the functioning of the 'whole', not just specific organisations, services or policy imperatives.

Technology-driven networks

Technology-driven network forms are consequent, it is argued, on the forces and relationships of production. When these forces and relationships change, so do the network forms. Many of the available studies look at collaborations driven by *technology* where leadership makes a difference to the success with which interorganisational networks can operate (for example, Volkoff et al, 1999, show that the successful development of interorganisational data systems is dependent on product champions working across organisational boundaries). In their study of local partnerships in US public administration involved in the joint adoption and use of geographical information systems-based technologies, Brown et al (1998) found that their measures for the presence of active leadership was a statistically significant – and positive – factor in all of their assessments of outcomes (albeit they are less clear about what sort of leadership). Fleming and Waguespack (2007, p 165) explore: 'What types of human and social capital identify the emergence of leaders of open innovation communities? Consistent with the norms of an engineering culture, we find that future leaders must first make strong technical contributions.' This suggests that, in the health and social care setting, technological innovation through networks is most appropriately led by practitioners (and this may also start to give more substance to the popular concept of distributed leadership).

However, beyond these technical contributions, they argue leaders must maintain support by:

> Two correlated but distinct social positions: social brokerage and boundary spanning between technological areas. An inherent lack of trust associated with brokerage positions can be overcome through physical interaction. Boundary spanners do not suffer this handicap and are much more likely than brokers to advance to leadership. The research separates the influence of human and social capital on promotion, and highlights previously unexamined differences between

brokerage- and boundary-spanning positions. (Fleming and Waguespack, 2007, p 165)

These issues have been examined. Bardach's (1998) analysis of his case studies led him to suggest that 'effective' leadership was important for network success, both in his interviewees' estimation and in his own research evaluation. Like Fleming and Waguespack, he distinguishes between facilitative – more neutral, consensus-building – approaches and advocacy approaches that are more partisan (and which may be readier to leave people out of coalitions). Bardach is not able to demonstrate the different conditions within networks for the efficacy of using each type of his identified approaches to leadership. However, using one of the frameworks introduced in Chapter 1 (see Figure 1.2), it seems plausible that advocacy styles would be more likely to be effective in individualistic or hierarchical networks, and facilitative styles more likely to be seen as legitimate in enclave-type networks.

Vangen and Huxham (2003, p 70) also note that the facilitative approach can co-exist with 'pragmatic approaches that, at face value, seem less consistent with the spirit of collaboration.' For instance, collaborative leaders seem to take an active role in establishing the purpose of the network, that is, they adopt what Bardach sees as an advocacy role, where 'power and influence can be exercised on the direction of the collaboration through definition of issues' (p 70). There are links here back to Grint's earlier leadership model, where leaders attempt to socially construct the wicked problem to be addressed, and forward to our discussion in Chapter 4 of the importance of issue framing. This observation brings a welcome breath of reality to the discussion; as they point out, leaders of collaborations have targets to meet, especially in UK public services, and have to actively avoid perceptions of failure or inertia. It chimes with our critique in Chapter 1 of many of the features of transformational leadership being aspirational, if not fanciful, in terms of the challenges faced by public services.

Vangen and Huxham's term for this advocacy stance, rather oddly, even allowing for dramatic effect, is 'collaborative thuggery'. Its characteristics are summarised in Figure 2.1. In the more detailed discussion, it transpires that this 'thuggery' is used by collaborative leaders to overcome the sorts of challenges outlined in Figure 2.1.

Figure 2.1: Towards 'collaborative thuggery'

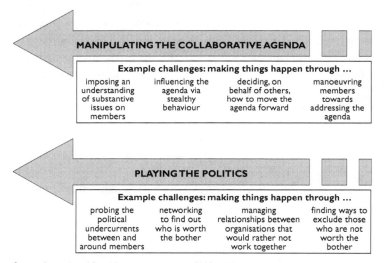

Source: Reproduced from Vangen and Huxham (2003, p 70)

They conclude that leaders of collaborative endeavours need to be adept at both facilitation and 'thuggery' and at managing the interaction between them: 'an overemphasis on either would not be likely to generate collaborative advantage' (p 73); in our view, boundary spanners need to be adept at both. Again, we shall return to some of these (presumably) thuggish – let us settle for the more neutral 'manipulative' – techniques in Chapter 4. More recently, various web platforms have begun to emerge to drive the creation of networks, for example, MindHive and the Business Portal (see the end of this chapter for relevant web links). As new entities, it remains unclear how technologically driven connections can facilitate what the literature suggests is a deeply relational practice regarding collaborative leadership.

With this qualification in mind, let us move on, then, to the attributes of facilitative collaborative leaders.

What the evidence suggests are attributes of collaborative leaders

One of the apparent paradoxes of the literature on the attributes of collaborative leaders is that while notions of leadership in collaborative settings seem to stress the importance of process, many of the necessary skills could be best seen as individualised traits. In other words, although this literature highlights the fact that leadership within collaborations is shared and relational, there is still a tendency to construct lists of personal competencies that individuals should develop in order to be successful inter-agency leaders. Moreover, many of these characteristics also cleave quite closely to charismatic notions of leadership. The reported importance of the relational aspects of collaborative leaders has prompted us to focus on the performative aspects of leadership as one of the emerging themes in Chapter 3. Williams (2002, p 118) concludes that 'there is a general view that the "real" business of partnership work is effected within the framework of ... personal exchanges. It is where difficulties are shared, aims agreed, problems sorted out, deals struck and promises made – all out of the public gaze.' This illustrates once more the difficulties inherent in leading and managing collaborations, and also the way in which these entities often rely on personal relationships and extensive action 'backstage'. One of the challenges faced for many adopting leadership roles in collaborative settings is that traditional approaches to development are still adopted in preparing individual for these roles.

As Osborne (2010, p 421) observes,

> ... the reality of contemporary public service management is that it is an interorganizational and collaborative activity, and requires the governance of complex systems and interorganizational processes. Despite this, training has often remained rooted in organizational needs rather than

embracing the requirement to develop skills in managing the complex processes of interorganizational, network and systems governance.

In order to ascertain just what it is that development programmes should be seeking to develop beyond these more traditional skills, Williams (2012) reviews the literature on boundary spanning and leading and managing in inter-agency settings. Table 2.2 sets out the findings of this review and the various attributes, skills and behaviours required of collaborative leaders. These attributes, skills and competencies are in addition to those required in traditional settings, and Williams argues that individuals should be trained as public managers first, and only then would they be ready to embark on a programme aiming to develop collaborative leadership skills.

A further interesting debate takes places within the collaborative leadership literature, which in a number of senses is highly redolent of the broader leadership literature, concerning the degree to which good collaborative leaders can be developed or whether they are born that way. Sarason and Lorentz (1998) talk of the need for collaborative leaders to

Table 2.2: Collaborative leadership competencies

Attributes	Skills	Behaviours
Collaborative mindset	Self-management	Stakeholder identification
Passion towards outcomes	Strategic thinking	Stakeholder assessment
Systems thinking	Facilitation skills	Strategic issues framing
Openness and risk taking		Convening working groups
Sense of mutuality and connectedness		Facilitating mutual learning processes
Humility		Inducing commitment
		Facilitating trusting relationships among partners

Source: Adapted from Williams (2012, p 134)

be 'paragons of virtue' or 'secular angels' in the sense that they need to likeable, but also tactful and not pushy (p 107). What is apparent is that boundary spanners are typically viewed as being outgoing, cheerful and extroverts, but also honest, respectful, highly moral, hardworking and persistent. Table 2.3 sets out some of the kinds of personal characteristics that are desirable in boundary spanners, drawing on work by Williams (2005). There is a danger in this context that boundary spanners begin to be viewed as some form of modern superwoman, as reflected on

Table 2.3: Desirable personal characteristics of boundary spanners

Personal attributes	Description
Respect for others and their views	Appreciating, comprehending and accommodating diversity and difference in people's perspectives and opinions. The key word here is respect, which does not mean agreement but valuing other people's right to their own views. It is also considered important also to look for opportunities to demonstrate this respectfulness, and to be tolerant of others' positions on various matters. Innate curiosity about the 'bigger picture' is thought to be an invaluable personal attribute
Honest, straight and trustworthy	Evidenced by being open in dealings with people, not being underhand or devious, or going behind their back
Approachable	This is about people who are accessible and not 'standoffish'; sometimes amusing, talkative and interesting
Diplomatic	Actors with well-honed political antennae who are careful in their use of language
Positive and enthusiastic	These people constantly champion and extoll the virtues and benefits of partnership working
Confident and calm	People who exude good judgement and are firm where necessary

Source: Adapted from Willams (2005)

earlier in the chapter. Indeed, gender is an interesting facet to consider in relation to the boundary spanner. Williams (2012) argues that women may be better placed to exhibit many of the kinds of desirable personal characteristics with greater ease than men. Although we should, of course, be wary of suggesting that any one gender is naturally better predisposed to particular sorts of activities.

An important point to consider is that collaborative endeavours may require different sorts of skills depending on the stage they are at and the kinds of activities being engaged in at that moment in time (Carey and Crammond, 2015a). Agranoff and McGuire (2001) suggest a life cycle approach to analysing collaboration, with four different categories for the behaviours of collaborative managers – activation, framing, mobilising and synthesising – and we extend this to add a further category of sustaining (set out in Box 2.5 below). In a similar fashion, Vangen and Huxham (2003) produce a four-stage model of embracing, empowering, involving and mobilising. On careful analysis, this schema seems to have quite a lot in common with Agranoff and McGuire (2001), and suggests that different types of competencies and skills are needed by leaders at different points in the life cycle of collaborative endeavours.

Box 2.5: Partnership life cycle

- *Activation* involves identifying the right people and resources for the efforts of the partnership.
- *Framing* includes facilitating agreement on leadership and administrative roles, helping to establish a culture and develop a structure.
- *Mobilising* is the aim of inducing enthusiasm to the collaborative and ensuring support from key external stakeholders.
- *Synthesising* involves helping to create productive and purposeful interaction between members of the collaborative.
- *Sustaining* means ensuring that new networks and collaboration are maintained beyond initial bursts of activity.

Another body of work has examined the idea that leaders of collaborative endeavours face peculiar stress arising from role ambiguity – and even conflict – because of the pressures placed on them both by their own organisation and the others with which they develop linkages (Robertson, 1995; O'Toole, 1998). Unfortunately, this research is not very extensive, although it is currently being developed in relation to literature on emotional labour (see Jelphs et al, 2016, for more discussion of this topic). In a study of women who took activist commitments into their working lives, Newman (2012) argues that boundary work is incredibly emotionally taxing as it involves operating multiple different affective registers at once. It can be hypothesised that boundary spanners often exhibit ambivalence in their accountabilities because of the potential conflicts and tensions in their roles, having pressures both from their employing organisation and from the organisations with which they develop links. There is a significant body of work on doctors who engage in corporate leadership or management roles and occupy particular forms of boundary work between the clinical and managerial worlds. Individuals occupying these roles often report extreme stress, not just because of the logistical difficulty that is associated with these jobs, but because they do not feel part of either camp (Dickinson et al, 2015a). Doctors are often viewed by their clinical colleagues as having 'gone over to the dark side' (Spurgeon et al, 2011), and yet they do not easily sit with their managerial colleagues either.

Overall, from their extensive consideration of leadership in networks, 6 et al (2006, p 157) conclude:

> [I]t is important to note that nothing in the boundary spanning literature shows that there is anything particularly distinctive either about the activities or about the skill sets of boundary spanners working between organisations when compared, for example, with colleagues working between departments within an organisation. Essentially, the same processes of initiation, negotiation, diplomacy, problem-solving and strategic development – and the same tact,

ability to move between accountabilities, energy to motivate others etc – are required in both settings. Indeed, much of the literature moves seamlessly from the inter- to the intra-organisational context.

This appears a slightly controversial position to adopt, albeit one that may usefully serve to demystify the concept of collaborative leadership. There may be nothing unique to collaboration regarding the leadership styles and skills that facilitate their success; rather, the difference may lie in the emphasis on particular elements of a more generic leadership model and in the specific contexts – and the challenges therein – within which they are deployed.

Those that challenge the conclusion drawn by 6 and his colleagues argue that it is indeed the very nature of these contexts that differentiates collaborative leadership. Armistead et al (2007, p 213) put this point clearly:

> [C]ompared to single organizations, working in partnership is of an order more complex and ambiguous, wherein inter-organizational relationships can be horizontal as well as hierarchical ... without necessarily diluting hierarchy ... where there is uncertainty about who leads and who follows ... where leadership can be represented by organizations rather than individuals within organizations ... and where governance arrangements (if they exist at all) may not really reflect leadership as it manifests itself in practice.

This is a persuasive argument for the network setting requiring distinctive styles of leadership, in particular, styles that call for more emphasis on aspects that would be less prevalent in uni-organisational arrangements. However, it must be remembered that this was not the predominant view of the collaborative leaders with whom they undertook their own research.

In reviewing the literature on leadership, it is clear that leadership continues to be seen as both critical and vexed. Poor leadership is often seen as the source of failed collaborative initiatives, yet how to lead effectively across boundaries and in collaborative environments remains unclear. Moreover, while the growth of policy networks continues to drive different forms of boundary-spanning activities, leadership tends to be framed as a skill set or critical competencies of individuals. These include mindset, an ability to see the whole picture, to think strategically, facilitate and coordinate.

Reflective exercises

1. Think of a collaborative leader you have encountered and consider to be effective. Do they demonstrate the kinds of competencies set out in this chapter? Are there other aspects that you think are important?

2. Think of a collaborative endeavour that wasn't successful. What was the role of leadership in this lack of success?

3. Think of a situation where you believe that effective leadership was responsible for a good outcome. What was it specifically about this leadership that resulted in a positive outcome, or were there any other factors that were also important? In what ways might this leadership have produced negative outcomes?

4. Drawing on the partnership life cycle set out in Box 2.5, what do you think the different capacities and capabilities of leaders might be at the different stages?

Further reading and resources

- For an inclusive and detailed overview of the many forms that networks take and the implications this holds for the practice of 'networks' in the public sector, see 6 et al's (2006) *Managing networks of twenty-first century organisations*.
- For a review of the boundary-spanning literature, see Williams' (2012) *Collaboration in public policy and practice*.
- For a review of practices associated with successful integrated initiatives, see Carey and Crammond's (2015a) 'What works in joined-up government? An evidence synthesis', and for a review of leadership for systems change in preventive health, see Fawkes' (2012) *Leadership for systems change in preventive health*.
- There are a range of national evaluations that all make reference to leadership and management in some form, including:
  - local area agreements (LAAs) (ODPM, 2005a, 2007)
  - LSPs (ODPM, 2005c)
  - Health Action Zones (Barnes et al, 2005)
  - Children's Trusts (University of East Anglia, 2007)
  - Health Act flexibilities (Glendinning et al, 2002)
  - National Sure Start Evaluation (National Sure Start Evaluation, 2005).
- For an interactive web resource on the challenges of collaborative leadership, visit Collaboration for Impact: www.collaborationforimpact.com/
- For more details on the Beyond the Bell example, visit www.collaborationforimpact.com/leadership-at-beyond-the-bell-great-south-coast-vic/
- For more information about Power to Persuade, visit: www.powertopersuade.org.au
- For more information on MindHive, visit: http://mindhive.org/
- For more information on the San Francisco Business Portal, visit: http://businessportal.sfgov.org/

3

Hot topics and emerging issues

Through a series of themed sections, this chapter explores three current and future key issues in management and leadership in inter-agency collaborations. Given the volume and breadth of literature concerning leadership and management, there are a great many potential issues we might have covered in this chapter, and selecting just a few areas to focus on has been a challenge. We have selected those that we believe are of greatest interest to those actively involved in collaborative working, namely:

- 'No more heroes': leadership as a distributed practice
- Boundary objects – a new space for leadership?
- Leadership as sense-making and performance.

'No more heroes': leadership as a distributed practice

As noted at the outset of this book, leadership has traditionally been viewed as a quality of individuals, that is, the charismatic leader, the 'great man' tradition (Lowe and Gardner, 2001; Brown and Gioia, 2002; Denis et al, 2012). However, with the growth of cross-boundary working in public sector management and various forms of cross-sectoral and cross-organisational collaboration (Rhodes, 1997, 2007), new concepts of leadership have necessarily emerged. Over the last decade or so, particular interest has grown in various forms of 'plural' leadership (Denis et al, 2012), which broadly refers to forms of shared leadership. These can range from shared leadership among a central team or elite group (who lead subordinates), to views of leadership as a collective process of interaction (that is, leadership as a collective practice, rather than a position). Shared leadership is thought to be particularly relevant in aiming to solve complex problems where no one individual will be able to provide 'the' answer (Osborne, 2006, 2010). Figure 3.1 sets out a continuum of plural leadership, from least to most distributed, and we have plotted on this case studies presented in the previous chapter. Below we explore this continuum in more detail.

Figure 3.1: Continuum of plural leadership

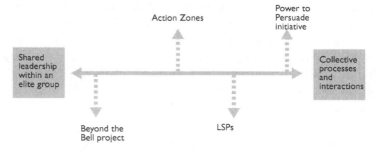

Source: Authors' own image

The central goal of plural leadership is to better assist organisations to 'integrate people, processes, structures and resources' (Crosby et al, 2010, p 200). Often, this occurs across boundaries, and is intertwined with the demands of collaboration (explored further in the next 'hot topic'). Here, relationships – rather than authority – are critical to 'getting things done'. To the left of the continuum sit practices where leadership is shared but still arranged hierarchically. For example, small teams of leaders may share responsibilities, but still operate through authoritative means to coordinate and organise the actions of subordinates (Brown and Gioia, 2002; Gronn, 2002, 2015). An example of this is the Beyond the Bell project, outlined in Chapter 2, where a central leadership group sets the course of action for local implementation groups. More distributive forms of leadership spread leadership duties within and across organisational levels or over time (that is, rotational practices) and even across interorganisational boundaries (Brown and Gioia, 2002; Edwards, 2011; Denis et al, 2012;

Fitzgerald et al, 2013), although they still tend to prioritise individuals in authoritative positions, compared to more radical conceptualisations of leadership, which we will discuss shortly.

Distributive leadership is seen as a way to enable complex, cross-boundary change with different actors taking on different roles over time. It is important to note that all leaders within leadership teams do not have to act in harmony for leadership to be recognised as distributed (Spillane and Diamond, 2007). A 'shared common root' can be enough to demonstrate that 'leadership is more about participation, and collectively creating a sense of direction, than it is about control and exercising authority' (Denis et al, 2012, p 254). In an extensive review of leadership practices, Denis et al (2012) distilled a number of key elements required to make distributive leadership work:

- consistent signalling by top management
- role interdependence
- good relationships and trust
- champions in key positions
- available resources.

Within the literature on distributed leadership, Denis et al (2012) note that shared leadership is often seen as intertwined with self-leadership. Self-leadership is seen as a prerequisite for shared or team leadership: 'a process through which people influence themselves to achieve the self-direction and self-motivation needed to perform' (Houghton et al, 2003, p 126). To the above list, we can then add:

- individual trust
- self-efficacy
- individual commitment (Denis et al, 2012).

As noted previously with regard to the leadership literature more broadly, much of the work on distributive leadership still emphasises individual attributes from which shared leadership can emerge, and focuses far less on the sorts of organisational conditions that it might flourish within (Burke et al, 2003).

At the other end of the spectrum are views of leadership as completely relational processes ('relational leadership'). Relational leadership moves entirely beyond 'uni-directional or even reciprocal leader/follower relationships to one that recognises leadership wherever it occurs' (Hunt and Dodge, 2001, p 448). This means that leadership is not restricted to a group of authoritative individuals, but takes a more radical view of leadership and organisations as 'human social constructions that emanate from rich connections and interdependencies of organisations and their members' (Uhl-Bien, 2006, p 655). In other words, knowledge exists and is created between individuals at all organisational levels, and effective leadership relies on both the creation and communication of this knowledge, but also on the connections that individuals have to one another. Here, leadership is completely liberated from role or position – it occurs in 'relational dynamics' between organisations within and across organisations (Uhl-Bien, 2006, p 655). Key actors or positions may play a role in leadership (that is, enacting, creating, influencing), but it is not isolated to those individuals or groups of individuals – it is a collective process.

While at the extreme end of views of plural leadership, relational leadership has much in common with systems perspectives that have gained interest in a wide range of fields concerned with solving complex problems (Berkes et al, 2000; Atwood et al, 2003; Best and Holmes, 2010; Campbell-Evans et al, 2014). Systems perspectives have emphasised the notion of 'adaptive leadership', which, similarly to relational leadership, views leadership as a practice and not as a position. Within an adaptive approach, leadership can be distributed to varying degrees, but leaders must manage ambiguity, interpersonal conflict and messiness (and possess the confidence not to be defensive in the face of these challenges) (Heifetz et al, 2009). The literature on adaptive leadership distinguishes between problems that are technical (clear issues, we know the answers) and adaptive (complex, multiple possible solutions) in a similar way to Grint's (2005a) distinction between tame and wicked problems (discussed in Chapter 1). Heifetz et al (2009) refer to the practice of adaptive leadership as 'choreographing the learning processes of others', while enabling and managing a productive state of 'disequilibrium' (that is, the messiness and ambiguity that emerges when no one perspective or individual's beliefs are privileged over another). Like distributive and relational leadership, adaptive approaches see gathering and synthesising diverse perspectives as key to solving problems (see Box 3.1).

Box 3.1: An example of adaptive leadership in school boards

Campbell-Evans et al (2014) provide a case study of an adaptive approach to leadership within the settings of local school boards, in an attempt to apply and understand Heifetz et al's framework in practice. They honed in on four elements of Heifetz et al's framework: the need for a 'balcony view', the role of leaders in orchestrating learning, the importance of diagnosing problems at the core of adaptive change, and the productive use of 'disequilibrium':

1. *The balcony view:* Adaptive leadership requires a 'balcony view', where one can get far enough above the day-to-day fray of an organisation to notice patterns. By doing this, we can distinguish between oneself and one's role – externalising conflict and identifying and sharing burdens with others. In Campbell-Evans et al's (2014) study, board members were classified as active on the balcony if they articulated a strategic role for the board, and showed evidence of bigger picture thinking in relation to their own or their board's responsibilities.

2. *Orchestrating learning:* An essential element in adaptive leadership is choreographing the learning processes of those in the organisation. In the case documented by Campbell-Evans and colleagues, this was done by creating induction manuals for board members, developing a 'buddy' system for new members, and creating an orientation year where board members are not given specific responsibilities but rather orientate to the board and its role.

3. *Diagnosing problems:* As Campbell-Evans et al (2014, p 546) suggest, 'An adaptive challenge is a complex challenge, and is often epitomised by

the fact that even the nature of the problem is unclear. Defining the problem then becomes a key step in the change process. The leader needs the right degree of tolerance of ambiguity.' Not acknowledging a challenge can prevent one from capitalising on opportunities that may exist as a result of it, or to overemphasise a problem when something simple such as greater clarification is needed before one can act. Campbell-Evans et al (2014, p 546) provide the following vignette to help elucidate this process: 'An item raised in general business at the Proflands board meeting observed by the researchers was risk management. Board members perceived the issue in different ways. One considered that the board should be thinking about risks to the school, per se: the potential loss of year seven students, competition from local schools, etc. A second was concerned about the school's risk management policy, the board's role in ensuring it was reviewed regularly, and whether or not the board should be endorsing the policy. A third thought that risk management was an operational matter, not a strategic one, and thus not the province of the board. The stark contrast of these three positions was not acknowledged by the chair. Instead, the apparent "resolution" was to accept the principal's suggestion that he take the matter to the expert group on Independent Public Schools within the Department of Education, for clarification.'

4. *Zones of productive disequilibrium:* Disequilibrium often arises from a diversity of opinions, but can also be centrally related to the adaptive challenge itself, because of the contradictions that can exist between people's beliefs, perspectives and understandings of the circumstances they face. It refers to the unease that arises when perspectives or beliefs collide within a group situation. The vignette above demonstrates a leader who avoided using this disequilibrium to explore different elements of the problem – choosing instead to put it to one side until greater clarification could be obtained. Hence, the goal is not to avoid conflicts but explore them, maintaining the group in a zone of productive disequilibrium.

Atwood et al (2003) put forward five 'keys' to guide adaptive approaches to leadership (see Box 3.2, where the five 'keys' have been refined in order to reflect the needs of joined-up government by Carey et al, 2016). These 'keys' align with many of the individual leadership competencies outlined earlier for boundary spanners, but place these competencies within a broader context regarding ways of working. Working in an adaptive way provides individuals with an appreciation of the 'whole' – the individuals, the organisations they make up and how they all relate to one another as a 'system' (Atwood et al, 2003). Through this, one can develop an awareness of the interdependencies between problems and propose effective solutions.

Box 3.2: Five keys to guide adaptive approaches to leadership

1. *Listening skills:* Different organisations or sectors speak different languages, work in different ways and experience different challenges.
2. *Start with questions:* Listening is a good first step, but questions are better. Questions help to gain deeper insights, and to understand the needs of others, for example, 'How do you see your professional practice?' 'What challenges do you experience that I may be able to help with?' 'What can I learn from you?' These types of questions lead to more innovative thinking.
3. *Approach with humility:* Each of us can only speak from our own experiences, which may differ significantly to those in other sectors. Different organisations are made up of vastly different professional practices, constraints and expectations. Remember, you don't know everything.
4. *Valuing difference and diversity:* Diversity has been a key ingredient for both a successful programme on the day, but also in the behind-the-scenes work to curate the event. As Atwood et al suggest, the greater the diversity of views gathered, the more likely it is that creative ways forward will be found. In addition to openly expressing opinions and experiences, this requires us to critically examine the differences

between our perspectives. Through this process, perspectives can be radically transformed.

5. *Follow through:* Whether on an individual, organisational or sector-wide level, change is almost always incremental. This means 'sticking with it', working through temporary impasses and accepting set-backs as par for the course.

Given that adaptive leadership is premised on the notion that answers do not lie within the domain of one individual, organisation or perhaps even sector, Atwood et al's skills have considerable cross-over with the use of boundary objects in crossing boundaries (which will be visited in more detail in the next section).

Adaptive approaches are gaining ground in a range of public services, from education to care (Campbell-Evans et al, 2014; Corazzini and Anderson, 2014; Snebold, 2015). However, such approaches present challenges. As Easterling and Millesen note (2012, p 21), an approach that relies on gaining and synthesising multiple perspectives can lead to protracted discussion with no decisive action: 'New and different voices at the table allow more possibility for disagreement, which in turn can stymie a group in moving to the concrete action that ultimately will make a difference to the issue at hand.' Porteous (2013) argues that adaptive approaches can still be top-down in practice, excluding communities from the problem-solving process. In other words, with any paradigm shift, challenges still emerge.

Which forms of plural leadership are most useful is highly context-dependent, both in terms of the problem to be solved and the organisational or team structure. Figure 3.2 provides an indication of what forms of plural leadership are most likely to be useful in different circumstances. However, it is worth noting that much of the work in this field is highly exploratory, and no firm rules or ingredients for success exist. Again we should be mindful of taking a normative approach to this form of leadership – just because it can solve some issues (or work in some contexts) does not mean that it will in all. Alternatively, new or hybrid forms of plural leadership could be developed which are context-specific (and therefore more likely to be effective and practicable). The key message again is that individuals need to experiment with different approaches to identify one that is most appropriate to both context and task.

Figure 3.2: Different forms of plural leadership

	Sharing leadership for team effectiveness	Pooling leadership at the top to lead others	Spreading leadership across levels over time	Producing leadership through interactions
Empirical focus	Mutual leadership in groups: members leading each other	Dyads, triads, and constellations as joint organizational leaders	Leadership relayed between people to achieve outcomes	Leadership as an emergent property of relations
Particularly propitious contexts	Teams (product development, change teams, and crisis teams)	Knowledge-based organizations	Inter-organizational collaboration, public services, and education	Knowledge-based organizations

Source: Denis et al (2012, p 215)

Boundary objects – a new space for leadership?

In response to the creation of complex collaborative environments and the need for individuals and organisations to work across boundaries, we have seen the emergence of 'boundary objects', that is, entities (organisations or groups) that deliberately sit across organisational and institutional boundaries. These boundary objects, or boundary spanners (Williams, 2002), are groups or collections of actors that create different ways of knowing for the purpose of moving cross-sectoral collaborations forward (Crosby et al, 2010). They act as 'structural beacons' (Oliver and Ebers, 1998; Williams, 2002) – building, guiding and supporting cross-sectoral collaboration: 'Boundary objects and their development help participants make sense of their world, what they may want to do with it, and why, and, in doing so, they ... help connect people, ideas and other actors into a way forward' (Crosby et al, 2010, p 205).

Hence, boundary objects or groups are an emerging form of leadership – building and supporting innovation. The idea (and importance) of boundary objects aligns with emerging arguments about the importance of 'flexian policy actors' (Smith, 2014). Flexian policy actors can move across organisational and sectoral boundaries with relative ease, communicating ideas in ways that make sense within different contexts, and guiding diverse actors towards a common goal. This means strategically adopting different approaches and language in different contexts. Smith (2014) and Carey and Crammond (2015b) give the example of providing policy advice (which may be discordant with dominant political views) in ways that are 'vague' or structured around the core values of governments in power in order to gain traction.

The act of leading, or perhaps more accurately the 'art' of leading, through the use of boundary objects is of course a complex one, necessitating particular relational skills. Not surprisingly, these skills intersect with those outlined earlier for plural leadership and effective collaborative practice. They also draw on notions of both individual and plural forms of leadership. Skills to communicate ideas across contexts are inherently individual, yet the very act of deliberately creating boundary objects (and the act of boundary spanning) draws on relational concepts of knowledge. Boundary spanners and objects support the notion that valuable knowledge exists in the interactions between groups, and that by facilitating the exchange of experiences and ideas, individuals at all levels begin to take on cross-boundary leadership roles. An important aspect of leadership within collaborative environments, or in boundary-spanning initiatives, is therefore 'sense-making' (explored in more detail in the next hot topic).

The very nature of boundary objects also means that informal leadership (which can lend itself to more radical theories and perspectives, such as relational leadership) is critical (Osborne, 2010; Head, 2014): 'informal leadership ... is especially important because participants often cannot rely on a lot of clear-cut, easily enforced centralized direction' (Bryson et al, 2006, p 201). This is due to the nature of collaborative practice, which includes many (and potentially changing) entities, power imbalances and differing levels of commitment from different organisations. Here, local leadership and willingness to champion collaborative endeavours is thought to be important. Foster-Fishman et al (2001) suggest that building 'relational capacity' is key to overcoming these challenges. Here, positive relationships are built across and within organisations – based on 'new and expanded' ways of working. They argue this should occur on three levels: positive internal working climates that need to be created that are cohesive and built on trust, followed by helping those working in collaborations to create a shared vision, and lastly, developing an inclusive culture. Moreover, because the contexts are constantly changing, collaborative capacities need to be continually assessed and developed, 'empowering communities to respond to new challenges by developing new competencies, new relationships and new solutions' (Head, 2014, p 148).

Hence, successful boundary objects are likely to hinge on the right mix of individual and plural forms of leadership – with key champions who possess certain skill sets, but also a recognition that knowledge is frequently relational (existing and being created in the interactions between individuals and groups engaged within a collaboration, regardless of their level or role). To solve complex problems, collaborative initiatives need to seek change in ways that are negotiated, influenced and enabled (rather than directed) (Carey et al, 2016) (see Figure 3.3), necessitating leaders within boundary objects acting as facilitators and brokers of differing forms of knowledge and practice (6, 1997; Davis and Rhodes, 2000; Keast et al, 2004). To achieve this, Atwood et al suggest leaders embrace the 'five keys' outlined in Box 3.2 above.

Leadership as sense-making and performance

A common feature in both Grint's accounts of leadership (see, for example, 2005a) and the adaptive leadership approach (Heifetz et al, 2009) is that there is an important role for the leader in shaping the meaning that is given to situations by others; that is, a significant part of leadership consists of influencing the sense-making of others. What these perspectives reflect are ideas originating in social constructionism (Berger and Luckmann, 1966), which are increasingly embedded in

Figure 3.3: Mechanisms for change in complex networks

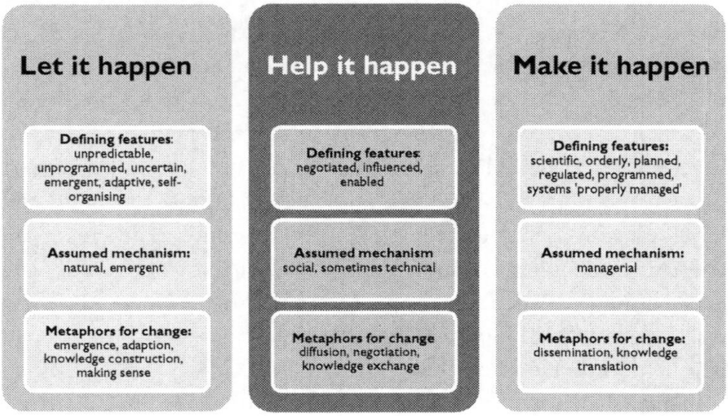

Let it happen	Help it happen	Make it happen
Defining features: unpredictable, unprogrammed, uncertain, emergent, adaptive, self-organising	**Defining features:** negotiated, influenced, enabled	**Defining features:** scientific, orderly, planned, regulated, programmed, systems 'properly managed'
Assumed mechanism: natural, emergent	**Assumed mechanism:** social, sometimes technical	**Assumed mechanism:** managerial
Metaphors for change: emergence, adaption, knowledge construction, making sense	**Metaphors for change:** diffusion, negotiation, knowledge exchange	**Metaphors for change:** dissemination, knowledge translation

Source: Adapted from Greenhalgh et al (2004)

leadership and organisational theory more generally. In this section we present a short introduction to social constructionism and sense-making. This discussion is important because Grint (2000, p 28) argues that:

> Leadership is the world of the performing arts, the theatre of rhetorical skill, of negotiating skills, and of inducing the audience to believe in the world you paint with words and props.

In so doing, he is describing the leadership role in sense-making as a form of performance. This section will also, therefore, explore the sorts of performances that leaders might give in order to shape the views of others. In both cases, it is worth being clear from the outset that our view of the role of the leader in collaborative endeavours is, in the terms used by Bardach (1998), more about advocacy (or, in our words, 'manipulation') than it is about facilitation (where we doubt that a 'neutral' position for a leader is possible even if it was desirable).

Social constructionism and sense-making

Social constructionism (see Burr, 1995) asserts that:

- our knowledge of the world is partial and very specific to the historic and cultural circumstances in which it is created or shared;
- this knowledge is co-constructed through interactions between people;
- knowledge (and the consequent social action) changes over time to produce numerous possible social constructions.

The theory suggests that the meanings we attribute to our experience (be they social problems or network objectives) are thus:

- *multiple*, because each of us has our own;
- *negotiated*, because we seek to find common ground with others;
- *contested*, because finding such common ground can be difficult;
- *transient*, because we are frequently discovering new meanings in these conversations and discarding old ones.

Social constructionism, therefore, suggests that human interactions have the power to shape the attitudes and behaviours of other members of organisations. In organisational theory, the particular term that has come to represent this phenomenon is 'sense-making' (see, for example, Weick, 1995), introduced briefly in Chapter 1. Box 3.3 summarises the seven distinguishing features of sense-making that Weick describes.

The importance of Weick's work in leadership is that it emphasises the potential for interventions by leaders to change the way in which organisational pasts, presents and futures are interpreted (for an example, see Pye, 1995). Beyond the organisation, social constructionism and sense-making also suggest that policy problems, for example, those 'wicked' (adaptive) issues that need to be addressed in collaboration, do not arrive ready-made, but rather, have to be described, defined and named in a process that is typically called 'framing' (Goffman,

1974). The way in which problems are framed – either nationally or locally – will also restrict the range of responses considered realistic.

Box 3.3: Weick's seven properties of sense-making

1. Grounded in the importance of sense-making and in the construction of the identity of the self (and of the organisation): 'Who I am as indicated by discovery of how and what I think'.

2. The process is retrospective in its focus on sense-making as rendering meaningful lived experience: 'To learn what I think, I look back over what I said earlier'.

3. Sense-making recognises that people produce at least part of the environment (for example, the constraints and opportunities) within which they are operating: 'I create the object to be seen and inspected when I say or do something'.

4. It stresses that sense-making is a social process undertaken with others: 'What I say and single out and conclude are determined by who socialised me and how I was socialised, as well as by the audience I anticipate will audit the conclusions I reach'.

5. Sense-making is always ongoing in that it never starts and it never stops (even though events may be chopped out of this flow in order to be presented to others): 'My talking is spread across time, competes for attention with other ongoing projects, and is reflected on after it is finished, which means my interests may already have changed'.

6. Sense-making is typically based on cues, where one simple and familiar item can initiate a process that encompasses a much broader range of meanings and implications: 'The "what" that I single out and embellish as the content of the thought is only a small proportion of the utterance that becomes salient because of context and personal dispositions'.

7. Sense-making is driven by plausibility rather than accuracy: 'I need to know enough about what I think to get on with my projects but no more, which means that sufficiency and plausibility take precedence over accuracy'.

Source: Derived from Weick (1995, pp 61-2), in Hardacre and Peck (2005)

In what ways is leadership a performance?

Let us return first to Weick's fourth property of sense-making as a social process. The use of the word 'audience', both here and in the earlier quotation by Grint (2000), suggests that one aspect of leadership is that of the performer telling a story that is being tailored to be plausible (another term used by Weick) to this 'audience'. In most accounts of leadership, attention is paid to the performer (leader) at the expense of the stories that they tell or the audiences (potential followers) that they address. In the next few paragraphs, we outline the practical benefits of focusing more on the stories and audiences in a context where we have already established (in Chapter 2) that an important apparent attribute of leaders in networks is *relational competence*. We argue that the attribution of *relational competence* (or, for that matter, *integrity* or *commitment*) to a collaborative leader is a consequence of the positive response of a range of audiences to the stories that they hear and read:

> Certain events are performances and other events less so. There are limits to what "is" a performance. But just about anything can be studied "as" performance. Something "is" a performance when historical and social context, convention, usage, and tradition say it is … from the vantage of cultural practice, some actions will be deemed performances and others not; and this will vary from culture to culture, historical period to historical period. (Schechner, 2003, p 38)

The origins of performance as an academic discipline lie in accounts of ritual within anthropology, specifically the rites and ceremonies that enact social relationships (Bell, 1997). One of the key ideas in this literature is that of *restored behaviour*, defined as the 'physical, verbal or virtual actions that are not-for-the-first-time; that are prepared or rehearsed' (Schechner, 2003, p 29). Broadly speaking, in this tradition the emphasis is on deliberate performance; that is, on occasions where the event 'is' a performance, for example, religious ceremonies or board meetings (this is a key point as we are talking about performing and not acting – think Rowan Williams, Archbishop of Canterbury, not Rowan Atkinson in *Blackadder*).

Effective ritual performance relies on the shared understandings of performer, co-participants and audience about the rules and purposes of the performance being given. Freeman and Peck (2007) use this approach in their analysis of a public board that, at least in its early days, struggled to be an effective ritual. As a consequence of these problems, the board took to having private pre-meetings (quite literally, rehearsals). The relevance to leading in partnerships is that if such rituals both serve to endorse the framing given to problems and to enact social relationships (see Peck et al, 2004), then leaders need to give careful consideration to the creation and maintenance of these fora. Indeed, many boards already acknowledge the benefits of innovations in setting and staging by organising, for example, member seminars within the timetable of board meetings. Nonetheless, given that such boards are also the place where *asymmetrical power relations* and *perceptions of legitimacy* may be played out (as in the case study reported by Freeman and Peck, 2007), then once again it seems it is the setting within which leadership in partnership takes place that gives the role its distinctiveness.

At the same time, Schechner (2003, p 29) argues that '[M]any events and behaviours are one time events. Their "oneness" is a function of context, reception, and the countless ways bits of behavior can be organized, performed, and displayed.' If much of the work of boundary spanners takes place in more informal settings, and attributions of *integrity* and *commitment* are essential to their positive impact, then this will call for one-off performances in tailoring a broadly consistent narrative that remains relevant to the interests of a range of audiences. This means significant discipline on the part of the leader. The great opportunity of performances by leaders that shape sense-making by an audience is that everything that s/he says or writes will have an impact. At the same time, the great burden of performances by leaders that shape sense-making by an audience is that everything that s/he says or writes will have an impact!

We think that there are three important overall messages that arise from this discussion (outlined in Box 3.4).

Box 3.4: Key messages about collaborative leaders and sense-making

- The role of leaders in shaping the meaning that partners attach to the network – in particular, in the framing of the problems to be addressed and their potential solutions – may be crucial.
- In intervening in sense-making, leaders need to give as much careful attention to their narrative and their audience as they may already do to their own performance.
- The consideration of formal meetings as rituals reveals some practical issues that leaders need to bear in mind in their design and delivery, especially as such events are central to creating and maintaining social relations between partners.

Peck and Dickinson (2009) set out an account of performance and leadership, and outline what a development programme that takes the kinds of ideas set out above would look like. They argue that leaders need to pay particular attention to three particular aspects of performance in delivering successful leadership:

- *Enactment* builds on the dramaturgical tradition (see, for example, Hajer, 2005). This facet pays attention to what leaders actually do and how they interact with others. It is the literal performance of leadership.
- *Narrative* refers to the kinds of stories that leaders relate, linking leaders with processes of organisational sense-making.
- *Audience* draws attention to the attributions of leadership made by those witnessing the performance, revealing that audience responses are diverse and only ever partially under the control of the performer.

These three factors comprise the E-N-A framework, which Peck and Dickinson assert are crucial in the primary purpose of the leadership performance, that is, the acceptance by an audience of the putative leader's legitimate authority to influence its sense-making. It is in the act of achieving or confirming the attribution of this sort of legitimacy that leadership lies. In their text they go on to set out how the E-N-A framework was used in a leadership development programme and the impacts that this had on those taking the course. Overall this approach was found to have a positive impact on the leadership of the individuals involved in the programme, particularly when compared to other approaches to leadership development (Peck and Dickinson, 2010).

Reflective exercises

1. What types of collaborative leadership are you engaged in (see Figure 3.2)? To what degree does this fit with your organisation or project's aims?
2. Reflect on a situation in which leaders were 'helping it happen' versus 'making it happen'. What were the differences in their leadership practice?
3. Which boundary objects can you identify in your organisation or team? Do these create or close down spaces for leadership?
4. Think about someone you consider to be a successful leader. In what ways might their actions be considered performances? How does this leader draw on sense-making processes (for example, what sort of stories does s/he tell)?
5. Using the E-N-A framework, think about a change that you are facing at the moment and how you might think about these different factors.

Further reading and resources

- For more on the changing nature of management and leadership in the context of government, see Eggers' (2008) 'The changing nature of government: network governance'; Carey and Harris' (2015) 'Developing management practices to support joined-up governance'; and Fung's (2015) 'Putting the public back into governance: The challenges of citizen participation and its future'.
- For an introduction to social constructivism, see Berger and Luckmann's (1966) *The social construction of reality*. See Grint's (2005a) 'Problems, problems, problems: the social construction of "leadership"' and (2005b) *Leadership*, which links leadership with concepts of social constructivism, and Peck and Dickinson's (2009) *Performing leadership*, which links these ideas to the performance of leadership.
- Weick's (1995) *Sensemaking in organizations* offers a seminal account of issues surrounding sense-making, and is a useful introduction to this area.
- See Goffman (for example, 1974) for further information on framing and the stages of performance.

4

Useful frameworks and concepts

Having diagnosed the many challenges inherent in leading collaborative endeavours and the inconsistencies and silences that exist in the vast literatures, in this chapter we turn to setting out a series of helpful frameworks and concepts as resources for those who are seeking to lead or manage inter-agency collaborations or create more effective leadership or management within an inter-agency context. In the course of this chapter we focus in particular on those that may be amenable to local leaders (as opposed to ones that arise from national policy, legal requirements and so on). McCray and Ward (2003) argue that without either a clear understanding of the tensions of policy – and its implementation at a local level – or a detailed analysis of professional roles in the light of political or economic factors, it is difficult to deal with the barriers to change that will arise (and this is a theme echoed in theories of adaptive leadership). It is therefore important that those who lead collaborative endeavours have the widest understanding possible of the context in which s/he is operating. The sections in this chapter again assume that, in practice, many (if not most) such leaders will be, in the terms explored in Chapter 2, 'active advocates' rather than 'neutral facilitators'. Unfortunately the bad news is that there is no one way to overcome the many challenges that managers and leaders of inter-agency collaborations face. As such, many of these frameworks and concepts should be used to guide local processes, and are often as much about what not to do as what to do in practice. There are no definitive answers in management or leadership, but we believe we draw on some of the most helpful guidance to be found for leaders and managers. Finally, it is important to stress that what follows can only briefly introduce some of the most helpful concepts, and readers may want to pursue further those ideas that resonate with them. Resources have been provided at the end of the chapter to aid this process.

Lack of a shared framework

Lack of a shared framework (of authority, accountability and procedures) between collaborators has long been identified as a source of significant challenge (and, in fewer cases, of strength, where difference is seen as diversity). This disparity is often raised in relation to the budget cycle and the use of financial resources (not surprisingly given that *resource exchange* is such a common form of network). In these circumstances, where many of the rules are outside of local discretion, the best approach that a leader can adopt may be to understand the nature of the difference and the problems and paradoxes that might ensue. There is some evidence in the literature that effective collaborations shape the organisational arrangements of the partners. This clearly takes time (and has been called 'negotiated order' by Emery and Trist, 1973). Nevertheless, it is perhaps partially frustration with the problems that arise consequent to these issues of authority, accountability and procedures within networks that prompt policy-makers to suggest solutions that move collaborations towards more hierarchical organisational forms. Yet such approaches may merely serve to delay the impact or to move the location of these problems (see Hudson, 2004, for a discussion).

Expectations, however, are more open to influence. It is worth, at this point, recalling the leadership model of Grint (2005a) introduced in Chapter 1. He argues that the consensus – such as there is – about a model of leadership is based on:

> ... a naive assumption because it underestimates the extent to which the context or situation is actively constructed by the leader, leaders, and/or decision makers. In effect, leadership involves the social construction of the context that both legitimates a particular form of action and constitutes the world in the process. If that rendering of the context is

successful – for there are usually contending and competing renditions – the newly constituted context then limits the alternatives available such that those involved begin to act differently. (Grint, 2005a, pp 1470-1)

Further, Grint argues that 'where no one can be certain about what needs to be done to resolve a Wicked Problem then the more likely decision-makers are to seek a collective response' (p 1478). This suggests that expectations – that is, the nature of the 'wicked' problem to be solved by collaborative working – can be shaped at a local level, albeit that the parameters of these expectations will be more or less constrained by national policy and local factors. The framing of the problem is crucial, for in the framing of the problem lies the potential for some solutions to be privileged and others marginalised.

Problem framing has been written about extensively in the broad policy literature (see, for example, Goffman, 1974; Schön and Rein, 1994; Oliver and Johnston, 2000), but some of the most useful and accessible work in recent years is that of Carol Bacchi (for example, 1999, 2009). Bacchi argues that problems are not merely neat representations of issues that exist 'out there' in a coherent way, and that in naming a problem it draws attention to the ways in which issues are given a shape, which has implications in terms of what can (or cannot) be done. This line of argument is not too dissimilar to the work of a number of other authors in the field, but what is different is the development of the 'what's the problem (represented to be)' approach that sets out a series of questions that individuals or groups can use to identify and scrutinise the effects of problem representations within specific policy areas. This list of questions is set out in Box 4.1. These could be used individually and collectively to analyse a specific challenge that a collaboration faces in order to work through the issue in a systematic way and to consider what a shared vision of the problem might be.

Box 4.1: Bacchi's 'what's the problem (represented to be)' approach

1. What is the problem (of 'problem gamblers/gambling', 'drug use/abuse', domestic violence, pay equity, health inequalities, etc) represented to be in a specific policy or policy proposal?
2. What presuppositions or assumptions underlie this representation of the problem? Identify binaries, key concepts and categories.
3. What effects are produced by this representation of the problem? Consider the following kinds of effects: how subjects are constituted within this representation, the limits imposed on what can be said and lived effects.
4. What is left unproblematic in this representation of the problem? Where are the silences? How would 'responses' differ if the 'problem' were thought about or represented differently? (Here it is useful to think about shifts in representation of the 'problem' over time and/ or across cultures.)
5. How/where are dominant problem representations produced, disseminated and defended? How could they be contested/ disrupted? Explore contradictions and discursive resources for reconceptualisation (re-problematisation).

In addition to Bacchi and Grint, there are two other ways of thinking about this topic that are illuminating: complexity theory and 'big windows and little windows'. We shall briefly look at each here.

Complexity theory has become one of the most fashionable ideas within organisational theory in recent times, as touched on in Chapter 1 (for an overview, see Sweeney, 2005). One of the most influential writers, Ralph Stacey (for example, 1999), has conceptualised the agreement/uncertainty matrix (see Figure 4.1). Within this matrix, the vertical axis represents, for our purposes, *agreement* between partners about the nature of the issues that the partnership is going to address. *Certainty*, represented by the horizontal axis, suggests how sure partners are about the cause and effect linkages, that is, assuming we are at 'A', doing 'B' will lead to 'C'. Where a collaboration leader is operating close to the bottom left-hand corner – where agreement and certainty between partners are high – they can usually draw on prior experience to inform action (this is the tame problem of Grint's matrix in Figure 1.2, which he argues requires management, not leadership).

However, as we have frequently noted, most collaborations deal with 'wicked' problems, where either agreement or certainty – or both – are absent. In Figure 4.1, Zimmerman et al (1998) have developed Stacey's original matrix to explore further the response to these wicked problems. Where there is considerable certainty, for example, about which outcomes are desirable, but much less agreement about how these can be delivered, they argue leaders are in the realm of political decision-making. In contrast, where there is high certainty that we are at 'A' and that doing 'B' will lead to 'C', but no agreement that 'C' is a preferred destination, then they suggest that leaders are in the domain of ideological negotiation.

In the absence of both agreement and certainty, Sweeney suggests that leaders are in the realm of complexity, and follows the advice of Margaret Wheatley (2001) in recommending that they build networks, enhance communication, work collectively and allow direction to emerge. Henry Mintzberg (see, for example, Mintzberg and van der Heyden, 1999)

Figure 4.1: The Stacey (1999) matrix developed by Zimmerman et al (1998)

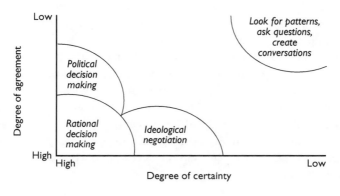

contends that we should look for patterns in participants' responses (and there are links forward to the discussion of culture here). Stacey argues that, in these circumstances, leaders should design opportunities for conversations (for example, stakeholder conferences, open space events) that facilitate new forms of consensus to emerge. These fora are presumably the settings within which leaders can pose the questions that Grint (2005a) maintains can shape the framing of the problem and the contours of the solution.

Uhl-Bien (2006) has suggested that within a complexity framework, leadership has three dimensions:

- *Adaptive leadership:* creative, adaptive learning from interactions between individuals or groups (that is, network dynamics).
- *Administrative leadership:* actions of individuals and groups in formal managerial roles who plan to accomplish specific outcomes. This refers to the actions of individuals who plan and coordinate organisational activities – structure tasks, engage in planning, build vision and acquire resources.
- *Enabling leadership:* which catalyses the conditions in which adaptive leadership can thrive and manage 'entanglement'.

Managing 'entanglement' is particularly critical, as administrative and emergent forces can work in opposition to one another. Here, the role of the leader is to balance these competing needs in such a way as not to allow administrative forces to crush emergent collaborative practices, and prevent collaborative practices from preventing organisations from meeting administrative objectives/requirements. Uhl-Bien (2006, p 306) argues that 'A role of enabling leadership at the strategic level then, is to manage the coordination rhythms, or oscillations, between relative importance of top-down, hierarchical dynamics and emergent complex adaptive system.' Hence, effective leaders protect from external politics and top-down forces, while ensuring resources are available and administrative goals are met. In this sense, they help to align organisational strategy and the needs of network actors (Uhl-Bien, 2006).

Another perspective on what leaders might do outside of the zone of rational decision-making – perhaps in the course of the conversations aimed at creating consensus – is to adopt Exworthy and Powell's (2004) *'big windows and little windows'* approach. Previous work on national policy by Kingdon (1995) suggested that an issue gets on the policy agenda when it brings together three 'streams':

* *the problem stream*, which outlines the nature of the challenge(s) to be resolved;
* *the policy stream*, which comprises the proposals to tackle the challenge;
* *the politics stream*, which consists of the interests of stakeholders.

The 'big windows' open – and policy is made – when these three elements are aligned within national government. Exworthy and Powell (2004) suggest that policy that requires inter-agency collaboration is best implemented when these three streams are also aligned at a local level (thus, the 'little windows'; see Figure 4.2).

Table 4.1 takes the ideas of policy-making and engagement suggested by Kingdon even further, highlighting the interconnections between structural components (that is, government departments) and discursive traditions. Carey and Crammond (2015b) use this analysis to argue that efforts to influence policy require leaders to navigate these interconnected dimensions successfully. This suggests that collaborative leaders attempting to gain commitment to action around a wicked issue need to use these conversations to frame the problem in such a way that it connects with the political predilections of the agencies involved, the structural realities of government departments and accountability mechanisms and, last, to position the problem in such a way that it comes complete with a policy solution that offers the prospect of progress and/or resolution, and not does exceed governments' perceptions of its ability to achieve change (that is, a problem that is too big or too complex). This links back to our discussion of flexian policy actors in Chapter 3. Flexian actors can weave together the structural and discursive dimensions across the three streams – helping to create

Figure 4.2: Congruence of 'big and little windows': vertical and horizontal dimensions

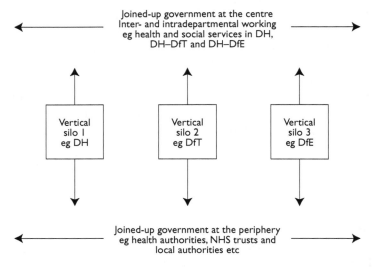

Notes: DH = Department of Health; DfT = Department for Transport; DfE = Department for Education.
Source: Adapted from Exworthy and Powell (2004, p 269)

'windows' for action. For example, the way they pitch a problem might align with the accountability structures in place, enable single departments to engage (but build towards a more connected vision), and utilise dominant ideological (or 'normative') positions at play.

Incompatible cultures and values

There has been much written about broader aspects of culture in health and social partnerships (see Peck et al, 2001; Peck and Crawford, 2004; Peck and Dickinson, 2008; Dixon-Woods et al, 2014; Mannion and Davies, 2015). This is because in discussions of collaborative working, one issue seems to recur more than any other: culture. Indeed, in the Francis report into the failings of care at the Mid Staffordshire NHS

Table 4.1: Structural and discursive dimensions of policy

	Streams		
	Problem	**Policy**	**Politics**
Structural dimensions	Accountability	Government silos	Community engagement
Discursive dimensions	Pitching the problem/solution	Non-linear policy	Normative reasons

Source: Carey and Crammond (2015b)

Trust (Francis, 2013), it is difficult to escape the conclusions that primary responsibility for this failure lay with the culture of healthcare organisations. Francis suggested that a fundamental cultural change is needed in the NHS to change it into an organisation that puts patient needs at its core, and many of the recommendations made in the report relate to changing the culture of the NHS to one that is shared. This reflects one of the themes within the broader collaboration literature where culture is often simultaneously to be both an aspiration for collaborations (for example, to change culture) and an obstacle (for example, conflicts rooted in culture). The literature suggests that this latter perspective is well founded. As we saw in the previous section, organisations may have such fundamentally different ways of framing issues, reacting to problems and interpreting procedural rules that bringing such different cultures together will lead to a situation of 'us versus them' (Marks and Mirvis, 1992).

Most accounts of culture assume what Meyerson and Martin (1987) call an *integration model*. This sees culture as something that organisations possess and which is therefore broadly recognisable and consistent across them. On this view, culture is an influence that can promote integration within organisations (thus two divergent cultures may need to be reconciled when organisations work collaboratively) and may be manipulated in relatively predictable ways in order to enhance integration. This is very much the kind of perspective present in the Francis report.

A second approach identified by Meyerson and Martin (1987) conceptualises culture as more pluralistic, with disparate cultures being held by different interest groups within the same organisation. On this view, culture is an influence which may once again inhibit integration (and thus partnership), but where the various cultures may be open to manipulation, in particular in relation to the ways in which they interact. This is the *difference model* of culture.

The third perspective discussed by Meyerson and Martin (1987) – the *ambiguity model* – considers it to be more local and personal than the other two, constantly being negotiated and re-negotiated between individuals and groups within the organisation. These patterns of creation and re-creation of culture may be influenced by the organisation within which and the interest groups between which they take place, but it is the one that perhaps offers the least prospect of predictable manipulation.

In their study of partnership development in Somerset, Peck et al (2001) identified the presence of all three of these levels of culture. Broadly, discussions with managers revealed an assumption of an integration model of culture; those with professional groups focused on professional difference (see below); and those with staff in localities suggested considerable negotiation and re-negotiation of culture consistent with the ambiguity model. In another account, Wistow and Waddington (2006) identify the *difference* model of culture in practice, while the collaborating agencies continued with the assumption that pursuit of an *integration* model would create an effective partnership; the authors report how the partnership process ran into difficulties due to 'basic incompatibilities, largely derived from the mismatch in cultures' (p 14). Wistow and Waddington summarise the characteristics of the NHS and social services partners (illustrated in Table 4.2). These are not uncommon characterisations of health and social care, and relate in part to the differing professional 'models' of care that are frequently typified as underpinning health and social care (again, we shall return to this in a later section). Clearly, therefore, deploying the Meyerson and Martin framework has potential for aiding both interpretation of and intervention in culture.

Is the management of culture possible? It appears that the difference and ambiguity views of culture offer less hope to the would-be

Table 4.2: Differences in characterisation of NHS and social services partners

NHS	Social services
Treatment	Care
National targets	Local needs
Must-dos	Local discretion
Universal services	Focus on vulnerable
Procedurally regimented and very top-down in style	Practical focus but has difficulty with strategy and planning

Source: Based on Wistow and Waddington (2006, p 14)

manipulators of culture than the integration model. Parker (2000) offers two conclusions from his review of the culture literature (and his case studies based in healthcare settings): the first is that 'cultural management in the sense of creating an enduring set of shared beliefs is impossible' (p 228); on the other hand, he suggests that 'it seems perverse to argue that the "climate", "atmosphere", "personality", or culture of an organisation cannot be consciously altered' (p 229). This is broadly the view adopted by us, although we also acknowledge – along with Bate et al (2000) – the poor track record of corporate cultural change programmes that do not simultaneously look at the prospects for changes in authority, accountability and procedures.

Is structural change enough to change culture? It would appear that structural change may not be enough. Indeed, in the short term at least, structural change can strengthen attachment to existing professional cultures (see Peck et al, 2002). Reviewing the extensive evidence on cultural change more broadly, Davies and Mannion (2013, p 3) warn that the Francis report would

> ... do well to tone down rhetoric around culture, be cautious about the idea of cultural uniformity, and be sceptical that top-down prescriptions will bring about the desired changes. Instead the emphasis needs to be on careful local nurturing, reaching for gardening metaphors in place of those rooted in ideas of engineering. Local contexts provide for organic,

home grown approaches that are sensitive to local histories and preoccupations, and real change requires detailed and sustained work on the ground.

What is clear from the work of Davies and Mannion is that culture is rarely as uniform as it might be assumed to be and can be difficult to change. With these caveats in mind, this section now briefly examines a range of tools for and approaches to interventions in culture in organisations.

In a systematic review of quantitative measures of organisational culture that have either been validated and used in healthcare settings or appeared to have potential for use in such settings, Scott et al (2003b) identify a total of 13 instruments (illustrated in Box 4.2). Scott and his co-authors (2003a) argue for the pragmatic selection of an instrument based on the purpose and context of any assessment. The researchers classify measurement tools as either typological (in which assessment results in one or more types of organisational culture) or a dimensional approach (which describes a culture by its position on a number of continuous variables). They identify four things to think about in utilising these tools:

- *Levels* – are you looking at the central core or more superficial manifestations?
- *Triangulation* – are you drawing messages following comparisons of data from various sources?
- *Sampling* – are you asking a representative number of staff?
- *Analysis* – are you going to explore the results by professional group or by geographical locality?

Box 4.2: Quantitative organisational culture measures

Typological approaches
- Competing Values Questionnaire
- Harrison's Organisational Ideology Questionnaire
- Quality Improvement Implementation Survey

Dimensional approaches
- Organisational Culture Inventory
- Hospital Culture Questionnaire
- Nursing Unit Culture Assessment Tool
- Practice Culture Questionnaire
- MacKenzie's Culture Questionnaire
- Survey of Organisational Culture
- Corporate Culture Questionnaire
- Core Employee Opinion Questionnaire
- Hofstede's Organisational Culture Questionnaire
- Organisational Culture Survey

Source: After Scott et al (2003b)

One framework of note is the Cultures of Care Barometer tool that has been developed to assist in the development of high quality care with the NHS (see Rafferty et al, 2015), and extensively piloted. The Barometer draws attention to the social processes at work within organisations that underpin trust, value and quality in terms of care outcomes. The tool works in two ways: it is a measurement to assess different cultures (and sub-dimensions of these cultures) and to see how culture varies within an organisation over time, and a way to prompt reflection on the underlying values involved in creating a culture. It can be used in one-to-one or group discussions with staff to stimulate dialogue about organisational culture. Box 4.3 sets out the details.

Box 4.3: Cultures of Care Barometer

The Barometer looks at three factors (which encompass 30 attitude items, which staff must rate) that tap into the tangible and the less tangible indicators of positive cultures:

- Resources and safety: for example, 'I have the facilities and equipment I need to do a good job'.
- Management and appraisals: for example, 'There is strong and visible leadership from senior staff,' 'My line manager provides support when I need it'.
- Values, ethos and responsiveness: for example, 'I regularly get feedback on what the organisation learns from incidents'.

The literature on organisational innovation has begun to emphasise the notion of narratives as a tool for shaping culture (Bartel and Garud, 2009). This is because culture is often regarded as a barrier to innovation: cultural values, norms and beliefs can become so ingrained that it becomes difficult for individuals to adapt to change. Consequently, cultural change is thought to require mechanisms that influence productive social relations and coordinated action across organisations. Innovation narratives are thought to promote the coordination of people and ideas across organisations, shaping practice through the power of language and a narrative about an innovation or required change. The idea is that these narratives can help translate ideas across space and time. Bartel and Garud (2009) suggest that innovation narratives ought to be flexible and present information, ideas or practices in a manner that is evocative. Consequently, they can be provisional in nature, 'capturing fragments of activities at a given moment in a less structured manner and without a clear plot' (Bartel and Garud, 2009, p 108). Innovation narratives may take the form of a new organisational vision or mission, which inspires and unites individuals within, or potentially across, different organisations.

Returning to our example of the integration of the NHS and social services, an innovation narrative might be used to unite this network of actors in a shared vision of change for improved care quality. In Table 4.3 we provide an overview of some of the ways in which innovation narratives can aid in cultural change and coordination.

Innovation narratives are an attempt to overcome the challenges that can arise when different individuals, with different perspectives (that is, from different parts of an organisation), are placed together for the purpose of creating change. A recent large-scale mixed methods study

Table 4.3: Innovation narrative, culture change and coordination

Aspects of the culture change process	Cultural change and coordination challenges	Mechanisms in innovation narratives
Genesis of novel ideas	Recombination of ideas from across the functional and hierarchical boundaries	Narratives serve as boundary objects to help in translation
Implementation	Real-time coordination of the activities of multiple constituencies	Provisional narratives allow for translation between multiple participants by prooting problem solving
Sustaining cultural change over time	Coordination of present and future initiatives with past initiatives	An organisational repository of narratives provides a generative memory that allows for the translation of ideas in ways that shape, but do not determine, ongoing innovation processes

Source: Adpated from Bartel and Garaud (2009)

conducted by Dixon-Woods and colleagues (2015) found that care, and care cultures, are inconsistent across the NHS, with 'bright spots' and 'dark spots'. Efforts to reform culture to address inconsistencies need, as Davies et al (2000) suggest, to be mindful not to disrupt areas where organisational culture supports high quality care. Similarly, Dixon-Woods et al (2015) note that it is important to build on 'bright spots' and the overall commitment to care they found among NHS staff. This, they suggest, involves modelling and reinforcing values and behaviours that underpin good practice. Box 4.4 outlines a number of strategies that might be used for creating and/or reinforcing positive cultures.

Box 4.4: Strategies for leaders and managers in creating and/or reinforcing positive cultures

Senior leaders should:

- continually reinforce an inspiring vision of the work of their organisations
- promote staff health and wellbeing
- listen to staff and encourage them to be involved in decision-making, problem solving and innovation at all levels
- provide staff with helpful feedback on how they are doing and celebrate good performance
- take effective, supportive action to address system problems and other challenges when improvement is needed
- develop and model excellent teamwork
- make sure that staff feel safe, supported, respected and valued at work.

Source: Dixon-Woods et al (2015, p 9)

Davies and Mannion argue that ultimately cultural change involves balancing tensions across a number of different dimensions (Box 4.5). Considering these tensions alongside the various available tools outlined above is likely to be the best way to bring about change to culture, although it is unlikely that such transformations will be as dramatic as some of the 'makeovers' of organisational culture reported within the literature (see, for example, Shirley, 2000; Bernick, 2001). Change is rarely easy to bring about quickly (and neither is rapid transformational change desirable), and the same model will not work in every place.

Box 4.5: Points to help senior managers and leaders facilitate cultural change

Cultural change needs a judicious blend of approaches that recognise tensions across several important dimensions:

- *Values (retention/ renewal):* many existing values are supportive of high quality care and need to be retained; others need to be challenged, changed or replaced.
- *Accountability (checking/trusting):* targets have a role in providing direction, focus and incentive, but high trust organisations can more easily learn and adapt to multiple competing demands.
- *Targets for change (external/internal):* local ownership of targets may be important; data used formatively rather than summatively have different effects.
- *Performance data (hard data/soft intelligence):* multiple sources of data, and a capacity and willingness to explore contradictions in these, are prerequisites for openness to learning.
- *Blame game (high blame/no blame/just blame):* blame is an insidious aspect of many cultures that creeps back in despite overt attempts to recognise its chilling effect.
- *Motivations (extrinsic drivers/intrinsic drivers):* too much focus on extrinsic rewards (salary, status, power) may crowd out intrinsic motivations (professional ethic, care, compassion).

Key senior management balances relating to cultural change include:

- Senior management style may need to vary between the transactional (getting daily tasks done) and the transformational (setting challenging new directions) depending on local performance, resources, and priorities.

- Management orientation may need to blend a corporate focus (to ensure cross-organisation alignment of values and goals) with a pro-professional orientation (that seeks to ensure proper account is taken of professional values around care).
- Middle management capacity needs to facilitate local change and performance without adding bureaucratic overhead. How much middle management, and of what kind, remains a perennial balancing act.

Source: Davies and Mannion (2013, p 4)

Finally, is there a clear link between organisational culture and organisational performance? From their exhaustive study in healthcare, Scott et al (2003b) decide that empirical studies do not provide clear answers, while noting that the available research is small in quantity, mixed in quality and variable in methodology (thus making comparisons between studies difficult), and more recent studies (see, for example, Davies and Mannion, 2013) concur with these conclusions. This is, of course, very different to the confident assertions of the authors of the 'culture cookbooks'. However, it seems counter to our intuition and our experience to deny any such link, challenging as this may be to prove to the satisfaction of researchers. Ultimately, consideration of both the literature and previous experience suggests that through reflecting on and intervening in organisational culture(s) with sense and sensitivity, partially through re-designing organisational structures when opportunities arise, managers and practitioners can achieve some change in that culture, while being aware that such interventions may well have unanticipated aspects.

Different professional discourses

One of the most frequently referred to difficulties in terms of health and social care collaborative working is the different professional discourses that exist in these organisations and which might serve 'tribal interests' (Hunter, 1996). Individuals are selectively recruited and socialised into professional groups that are essentially self-interested. Such groups will aim to protect themselves against others – professional identity often constitutes a valued part of an individual's personal identity (Evetts, 1999). This process of socialisation encompasses place, education, training and everyday experiences. In terms of education, professionals are not simply educated in terms of formal skills, but also less tangible 'informal' skills. This might include exposing individuals to the particular values, cultures, language and norms that tend to be associated with that profession. Via these processes individuals become part of a particular professional discourse providing a social boundary that defines what can be said about a specific topic. They become institutionalised into particular ways of sense-making (and thus behaving) (for examples of the divergent stories of their theory and practice told by professional groups working in mental health teams in London, see Norman and Peck, 1999). The teamworking book in this series (see Jelphs et al, 2016) provides further discussion about different professional discourses within teams, so we say little more about this topic here, with the exception of a final point regarding leadership and professional discourses.

One implication of the existence of these different professional discourses is that they are constituted by professionals who may have a high degree of influence or power within their context (such as clinicians), even though they may not occupy a position of formal authority (and are good examples of Lipsky's street-level bureaucrats). Thus, collaborations need to seek to engage the most appropriate individuals to lead or manage certain procedures at specific times, and often these will be individuals who may not always be associated with institutionalised roles.

Within this context, the role of dominant professionals, and particularly doctors, is of key importance. In Mintzberg's (1979, p 372) words, professional bureaucracies, such as those providing healthcare, 'are not integrated entities. They are collections of individuals who join to draw on the common resources and support services but otherwise want to be left alone.' Professionals are characterised as having a high degree of autonomy and the ability to resist calls for greater integration (Dickinson et al, 2013, 2015b). In this context, change is the product of 'successive negotiations [which] take place through a process of partisan mutual adjustment and as a plurality of interest groups operate in decision making areas' (Pettigrew et al, 1992, p 14). In developing this nuanced picture of professional collaboration within healthcare organisations, Denis et al (1999) emphasised three features of collaboration: emergent operating units; differentiated professional influence; and diluted managerial control.

Emergent operating units describe the distinctive forms of coordination among professionals that are associated with different categories of patient–group complexity. Whatever the source of complexity, medical control tends to dominate these operating units. In some cases this takes the form of a hierarchical model, while in others a key coordination mechanism is 'mutual adjustment among professionals' (Denis et al, 1999, p 109). Informal ongoing interactions between professionals are influenced by a range of factors, including tacit rules, mutual trust and 'intrinsic power relationships and incentives', and together produce the stable 'negotiated order' of emergent operating units (Denis et al, 1999, p 110). The operating unit 'is the key part of a professional organization because it is here that critical decisions about the content of work are made by professionals' (p 109). They argue that these semi-autonomous operating units form the de facto elementary structures of healthcare organisations, which are dominated by doctors whose knowledge makes them the de facto team leaders.

This concept has been developed under the 'microsystem' label and has emerged as a focus for clinical quality improvement work (Institute of Medicine, 2001; Nelson et al, 2002). Returning to organisational performance, the traditional autonomy over work practices exercised by senior clinicians has led to wide variations in medical practice, for example, the volume of healthcare provided that cannot be justified in terms of efficacy (Glover, 1938; Wennberg et al, 1987). The actions of these 'unofficial' leaders set a precedent in terms of what is acceptable within particular times and spaces. In order to change internal processes, these professional leaders must be engaged; this will give a clear and symbolic gesture to other members of that profession.

The challenges that follow from the power that resides in such street-level bureaucrats are compounded for leaders by the divergence in professional discourses. Fitzgerald et al (1999) illustrate this well in a study that set out to examine the adoption of clinical change within the acute hospital sector, and to identify the 'scientific' and 'non-scientific' factors shaping this adoption. In summary, the most evidence-based change was the least adopted and the least evidence-based change was the most adopted. They identify five key findings from this study and five implications for organisations (reproduced in Table 4.4). In essence, however, the research provides compelling support for the suggestion that it is in the processes of organising by leaders that the opportunities for change reside when working with professional groups.

This position is supported by an innovative study undertaken by Sullivan and colleagues (2012), who sought to understand different interpretations of leadership for collaboration. They discovered that leaders were not passive recipients of mandated governance changes, but rather were 'situated agents'. Leaders brought structure and agency (concepts outlined in Chapter 1) together, working within particular contexts but actively participating in design and action. That is, they acted as agents in this process, willingly pursuing their own goals. As a result, leaders embedded in the same governance structures interpreted their roles differently, and acted differently in accordance with this. As described in the previous chapter, context is often 'considered to be something that is 'outside' … that shapes the actions of … actors', yet, context and action are interdependent (Giddens, 1984; Newman, 2013). Sullivan et al (2012) found that leaders used past experience and anticipated outcomes to appraise challenges and chart a course of action. Hence, while we have argued that 'great man' theories of leadership are now redundant, the importance and centrality of individuals and their agency remains crucial to leadership in collaborative environments.

Hence, it seems that simple interventions – such as co-location of professionals – will not be sufficient to deliver the desired outcomes with regard to collaboration and partnerships. Rather, more subtle engagement with professional cultures and ways of sense-making will need to be combined with innovations in patterns of authority, accountability and procedure in order to achieve the benefits for patients, clients and the public to which collaborations aspire. In addition to the guidance set out in this chapter, the Advanced Leadership Institute has developed a range of tools to assist in coping

Table 4.4: The findings and implications of research by Fitzgerald et al on adoption of evidence-based practice

Finding 1	There was no strong relationship found between the strength of the evidence base and the rate of adoption of the innovation
Implication	Linear models of implementation are seriously misleading and are likely to lead to serious implementation deficits
Finding 2	Scientific evidence is in part a social construction as well as 'objective' data
Implication	There is no such entity as 'the body of evidence' but rather competing bodies of evidence available
Finding 3	There are different forms of evidence differentially accepted by different individuals and occupational groups
Implication	The intergroup issues also need to be addressed explicitly through the construction of linking bodies which bring the different groups involved in the implementation together, preferably within a learning environment and outside the busy daily routine
Finding 4	The data identify specific organisational and social factors that affect the career and outcome of clinical change issues
Implication	The most effective implementation strategies may combine top-down pressure and bottom-up energy
Finding 5	The upper tiers of the NHS, healthcare purchasers, Research and Development and the general management process played only a marginal role in the change process
Implication	There is a need to embed change within the professions themselves

Source: Summarised from Fitzgerald et al (1999)

with change and to be effective (see Easterling and Millesen, 2012). Table 4.5 provides an overview of available resources from the Institute for leaders.

Table 4.5: Insights and tools for leaders to cope with organisational change

Tool	Description
Personal History Timeline	An activity that allows participants to assess the present and future by looking critically at the past. Participants plot and analyse events at both an internal and external level. It allows a group to create a common reality and a common vision
Hold in Trust	A concept that allows leaders to identify the origins of their own development and how their character has formed. It promotes an awareness of civic trusteeship and the obligation to give back. It provides a foundation for adaptive leadership skills
Ladder of Inference	A tool that helps individuals and teams clarify problems, diagnose why the problems exist, and develop effective solutions. It builds consensus and ownership among a group when resolving the problem
Seven-Element Model of Conflict Resolution and Negotiation	A negotiation tool to resolving conflict in a collaborative manner. It allows the group to maintain trust and communication while resolving the conflict
Procedural Agreement	A planning tool that lays out the process by which a group will work, function, negotiate, problem solve, and reach its goal
Anger Cycle	A process that enables leaders to not become hostage to emotion. It helps the leader respond responsibly and respectfully in volatile, heated situations

Source:'Diversifying civic leadership:What it takes to move from "new faces" to adaptive problem solving', D. Easterling and J.L. Millesen, *National Civic Review*, 2012, vol 101, pp 20-6, © Academy of Management, reprinted by permission of Taylor & Francis Ltd, www.tandfonline. com on behalf of the Academy of Management

Reflective exercises

1. Think about an issue you or your organisation wants to address. How is the issue represented (see Box 4.1), and how might you represent it in a way that links together different policy streams (see Figure 4.2) to help open a 'policy window'?
2. Thinking about the issue from question 1, what are the structural and discursive elements of this issue?
3. Think about a collaboration you have experienced or have read about. Which of Meyerson and Martin's perspectives of culture are present? What practical implications does this have?
4. Investigate some of the organisational culture measures set out in this chapter, and think about which are most appropriate to a collaboration you know. If you can, use this as a measure. What does this tell you about culture?
5. Think about a collaboration you have experience of or have read about. Which different professional cultures are present? What implications do they have for joint working?

Further reading and resources

- For key readings about culture, Peck and Dickinson's (2009) *Performing leadership* and Davies and Mannion's (2013) 'Will prescriptions for cultural change improve the NHS?' may be particularly helpful.
- Useful websites and tools include:
  - The Culture of Care Barometer: www.england.nhs.uk/wp-content/uploads/2015/03/culture-care-barometer.pdf
  - The Wisconsin Advanced Leadership Institute toolkit, developed by Ki ThoughtBridge: www.kithoughtbridge.com/
  - Aston Organisation Development is a spin-out company from Aston Business School that hosts a wealth of resources including culture resources: www.astonod.com/

5

Recommendations for policy and practice

It would be to ignore the richness of the preceding discussion to try at this stage to draw out a simple set of lessons – to construct a cookbook after the banquet! As we have noted, there are no easy answers when it comes to the leadership and management of inter-agency collaboration. Therefore many of our recommendations have a distinct flavour: the best way to support leaders and managers is often to allow them to take responsibility for finding ways to work through challenges in a way that is appropriate for that locality. This is not to say that it doesn't matter if the broader context does not support collaborative working; it patently does, and we can learn from history about the many different initiatives and policies that have ultimately served to make collaborative working an even greater challenge. However, the evidence also suggests that we cannot just bring about high quality collaboration through changes to the macro environment; what happens locally plays an incredibly important part in making this happen.

Ultimately the challenges, summaries and frameworks we have set out in this text do lead us to make a set of practical recommendations and potential warnings, both for policy and for practice.

For policy-makers

• Although effective leadership and management do have a significant impact on the functioning of inter-agency collaborations, it is important that leaders' roles are not overstated, and that we are realistic about what types of leadership and management can produce what kinds of results in what sets of circumstances.

- Although it is often suggested that leaders and managers of collaborative working need skills and attributes distinct from those operating in more traditional settings, this distinction can be overstated; there are also significant overlaps in the types of tasks and challenges that both sets of leaders and managers will face, and these should not be underestimated. This has clear implications for the training and development of these individuals where understanding of the contexts for and nature of collaborative endeavours – and thus the sense-making and performance that may be most effective – may be as important as the skills and attributes themselves.

- Although formal governance structures are important to some types of settings, we should be wary of the instrumental claims that are made for these processes. Power does not simply reside at the executive level, which means we need to think through in more detail about how it may be exercised to bring about change. In particular, we need to recognise that power and leadership exist at all levels, and often reside in the interactions between individuals.

- The importance and implications of the interaction between political, community and organisational leadership should not be underestimated within collaborative settings. We need to be clearer about what these roles entail and how these leaders go about coordinating their activities.

For boundary spanners

While the literature on boundary-spanning practices, and leadership, is nascent, several lessons emerge:

- It is clear that a diversity of perspectives is needed around the table for a boundary-spanning effort to be effective. Through this, leaders can better gain a sense of the 'whole' system, which the boundary-spanning entities seeks to unite or change.

- There is a need to give explicit attention to building the relational capacity of those working as boundary spanners and with partner organisations. This links in with the first recommendation, in that we can only gain important contextual knowledge about the 'whole' by engaging constructively with a diversity of actors, requiring deft interpersonal and communication skills.

- Leaders should develop their capacity to help diverse actors engage in 'sense-making' with regard to the structure of the system or network, the characteristics of the problem and potential solutions.

For local organisations and front-line services

- There is a need to be clear about what types of drivers are present in any collaboration. These are important to establish as they influence the form that any collaboration takes and the difficulties that it may encounter.

- Different sorts of collaboration require different types of management and leadership, and it is important to consider the aims of the partnership and the types of tasks that they have been set up to address (as both these factors will influence the nature of management and leadership which will be most effective within these settings).

- Regardless of network form, different management and leadership attributes will prove more effective at certain points within the partnership life cycle than others.

- When asked to work collaboratively, it is useful for agencies to reflect on the ways in which they and their partners organise themselves and the different values and rituals that are privileged in these organisations. It is important to think through the settlement that will be reached between partners as this has implications for form and the ways in which power may be effectively executed.

Above all, the (often very theoretical) discussions and frameworks in this book suggest that managing and leading inter-agency collaboration is a set of difficult, intricate tasks. Rather than falling for the 'easy answers' of the management cookbooks, we hope that this attempt to synthesise and explore the evidence will give a more nuanced, and hopefully more useful, insight.

References

6, P. (1997) *Holistic government*, London: Demos.

6, P., Goodwin, N., Peck, E. and Freeman, T. (2006) *Managing networks of twenty-first century organisations*, Basingstoke: Palgrave.

6, P., Leat, D., Seltzer, K. and Stoker, G. (2002) *Towards holistic governance: The new reform agenda*, Basingstoke: Palgrave.

Addicott, R., McGivern, G. and Ferlie, E. (2007) 'The distortion of a managerial technique? The case of clinical networks in UK health care', *British Journal of Management*, vol 18, pp 93-107.

Agranoff, R. and McGuire, M. (2001) 'Big questions in public network management research', *Journal of Public Administration Research and Theory*, vol 11, pp 295-326.

Ahearne, M., Lam, S.K. and Kraus, F. (2014) 'The role of social capital: middle managers' adaptive strategy implementation', *Strategic Management Journal*, vol 35, no 1, pp 68-87.

Aldrich, H. and Herker, D. (1977) 'Boundary spanning roles and organization structure', *The Academy of Management Review*, vol 2, pp 217-30.

Alford, J. and O'Flynn, J. (2012) *Rethinking public services: Managing with external providers*, Basingstoke: Palgrave Macmillan.

Alimo-Metcalfe, B. (1998) *Effective leadership*, London: Local Government Board.

Alvesson, M. and Sveningsson, S. (2003) 'The great disappearing act: difficulties in doing "leadership"', *Leadership Quarterly*, vol 14, pp 359-81.

Anderson-Wallace, M. (2005) 'Working with structure', in E. Peck (ed) *Organisational development in healthcare: Approaches, innovations, achievements*, Abingdon: Radcliffe Medical Publishing, pp 167-86.

Armistead, C., Pettigrew, P. and Aves, S. (2007) 'Exploring leadership in multi-sectoral partnerships', *Leadership*, vol 3, pp 211-30.

Atwood, M., Pedler, M., Pritchard, S. and Wilkinson, D. (2003) *Leading change: A guide to whole of systems working*, Bristol: Policy Press.

Bacchi, C. (1999) *Women, policy and politics*, London: Sage.

Bacchi, C. (2009) *Analysing policy: What's the problem represented to be?*, London: Pearson Education.

Balloch, S. and Taylor, M. (eds) (2001) *Partnership working: Policy and practice*, Bristol: Policy Press.

Bardach, E. (1998) *Getting agencies to work together: The practice and theory of managerial craftsmanship*, Washington, DC: Brookings Institute.

Barnes, M., Sullivan, H. and Matka, E. (2004) *The development of collaborative capacity in Health Action Zones. A final report from the national evaluation*, Birmingham: University of Birmingham.

Barnes, M., Bauld, L., Benzeval, M., Judge, K., Mackenzie, M. and Sullivan, H. (2005) *Health Action Zones: Partnerships for health equity*, London: Routledge.

Barrett, G., Sellman, D. and Thomas, J. (eds) (2005) *Interprofessional working in health and social care: Professional perspectives*, Basingstoke: Palgrave.

Bartel, C.A. and Garud, R. (2009) 'The role of narratives in sustaining organizational innovation', *Organization Science*, vol 20, pp 107-17.

Bass, B. (1960) *Leadership, psychology, and organizational behaviour*, New York: Harper.

Bass, B. (1974) *Bass and Stogdill's handbook of leadership: Theory, research and managerial applications*, New York: Free Press.

Bass, B. (1990) *Bass and Stogdill's handbook of leadership: Theory, research and managerial applications*, New York: Free Press.

Bate, P., Khan, R. and Pye, A. (2000) 'Towards a culturally sensitive approach to organizational structuring: where organization design meets organization development', *Organization Science*, vol 11, pp 197-211.

Bell, C. (1997) *Ritual: Dimensions and perspectives*, Oxford: Oxford University Press.

Bennis, W.G. (1994) *On becoming a leader*, New York: Perseus Press.

Berger, P.L. and Luckmann, T. (1966) *The social construction of reality: A treatise its the sociology of knowledge*, Garden City, NY: Anchor Books.

Bernick, C.L. (2001) 'When your culture needs a makeover', *Harvard Business Review*, vol 79, pp 53-61.

Berkes, F., Colding, J. and Folke, C. (2000) 'Rediscovery of traditional ecological knowledge as adaptive management', *Ecological Applications*, vol 10, p 1251.

Best, A. and Holmes, B. (2010) 'Systems thinking, knowledge and action: towards better models and methods', *Evidence & Policy: A Journal of Research, Debate and Practice*, vol 6, pp 145-59.

Bevan, G., Karanikolos, M., Exley, J., Nolte, E., Connolly, S. and Mays, N. (2014) *The four health systems of the United Kingdom: How do they compare?*, London: The Health Foundation and Nuffield Trust.

Bevan, H. (2005) 'On the challenge of reform', Leeds: NHS Institute for Innovation and Improvement (www.institute.nhs.uk/quality_and_value/introduction/article_14.html).

Blake, R. and Moulton, J. (1965) 'A 9,9 approach for increasing organizational productivity', in M. Sherif (ed) *Intergroup relations and leadership*, New York: Wiley.

Boje, D. and Dennehey, R. (1999) *Managing in a post-modern world*, Dubaque, IA: Kendall-Hunt.

Bolden, R. and Gosling, J. (2006) 'Is the NHS Leadership Qualities framework missing the wood for the trees?', in A. Casbeer, A. Harrison and A. Mark (eds) *Innovations in health care: A reality check*, Basingstoke: Palgrave.

Brandsen, T., van de Donk, W. and Putters, K. (2005) 'Griffins or chameleons? Hybridity as a permanent and inevitable characteristic of the third sector', *International Journal of Public Administration*, vol 28, pp 749-65.

Briggs Myers, I. (2000) *Introduction to type*, Oxford: Oxford Psychologists Press.

Brown, M.E. and Gioia, D.A. (2002) 'Making things click: Distributive leadership in an online division of an offline organization', *The Leadership Quarterly*, vol 13, pp 397-419.

Brown, M.M., O'Toole, L.J. and Brundley, J.L. (1998) 'Implementing information technology in government: an empirical assessment of the role of local partnerships', *Journal of Public Administration Research and Theory*, vol 8, pp 499-525.

Bryman, A. (1992) *Charisma and leadership in organizations*, London: Sage Publications.

Bryson J., Crosby B. and Middleton Stone, M. (2006) 'The design and implementation of cross-sectoral collaborations: Propositions from the literature', *Public Administration Review*, vol 66, pp 44-55.

Burke, C., Friore, S. and Salas, E. (2003) 'The role of shared cognition in enabling shared leadership and team adaptability', in J. Pearce and J. Conger (eds) *Shared leadership: Reframing the hows and whys of leadership*, Thousand Oaks, CA: Sage, pp 103-22.

Burr, V. (1995) *An introduction to social constructionism*, London: Routledge.

Cameron, A., Lart, R., Bostock, L. and Coomber, C. (2012) *Factors that promote and hinder joint and integrated working across the health and social care interface*, London: Social Care Institute for Excellence.

Campbell-Evans, G., Gray, J. and Leggett, B. (2014) 'Adaptive leadership in school boards in Australia: an emergent model', *School Leadership & Management*, vol 34, pp 538-52.

Carey, G. and Crammond, B. (2015a) 'What works in joined-up government? An evidence synthesis', *International Journal of Public Administration*, pp 1-10.

Carey, G. and Crammond, B. (2015b) 'Action on the social determinants of health: Views from inside the policy process', *Social Science & Medicine*, vol 128, pp 134-41.

Carey, G. and Harris, P. (2015) 'Developing management practices to support joined-up governance', *Australian Journal of Public Administration*.

Carey, G., Landvogt, K. and Barraket, J. (2016) *Creating and implementing public policy: Cross-sectoral debates*, London: Routledge.

Carnevale, D. (2003) *Organizational development in the public sector*, Boulder, CO: Westview Press.

Chapman, C., Getha-Taylor, H., Husar Holmes, M., Jacobson, W.S., Morse, R.S. and Sowa, J.E. (2015) 'How public service leadership is studied: An examination of a quarter century of scholarship', *Public Administration*.

Collins, J. (2001) *Good to great: Why some companies make the leap and others don't*, London: Random House.

Corazzini, K.N. and Anderson, R.A. (2014) 'Adaptive leadership and person-centered care: A new approach to solving problems', *North Carolina Medical Journal*, vol 75, no 5, pp 352-4.

Craig, D. (2004) *Building on partnership: Sustaining local collaboration and devolved coordination*, LPG Research Paper No 15, Auckland: University of Auckland.

Crosby, B., Mclaughlin, K. and Chew, C. (2010) 'Leading across frontiers', in S. Osborne (ed) *The new public governance*, New York: Routledge, pp 200-22.

Crouch, C. (2005) *Capitalist diversity and change: Recombinant governance and institutional entrepreneurs*, Oxford: Oxford University Press.

Davis, G. and Rhodes, R.A.W. (2000) 'From hierarchy to contracts and back again: Reforming the Australian Public Service', in M. Keating, J. Wanna and P. Weller (eds) *Institutions on the edge*, Melbourne, VIC: Allen & Unwin, pp 74-98.

Davies, H.T.O. and Mannion, R. (2013) 'Will prescriptions for cultural change improve the NHS?', *British Medical Journal*, vol 346.

Davies, H.T.O., Nutley, S. and Mannion, R. (2000) 'Organisational culture and quality of health care', *Quality in Health Care*, vol 9, pp 111-19.

Davies, J. (2004) '"Conjuncture or disjuncture?", An institutionalist analysis of local regeneration partnerships in the UK', *International Journal of Urban and Regional Research*, vol 28, pp 570-85.

Degeling, P. (1995) 'The significance of "sectors" in calls for urban health intersectorialism: an Australian perspective', *Policy & Politics*, vol 23, pp 289-301.

Denis, J.-L., Langley, A. and Sergi, V. (2012) 'Leadership in the plural', *The Academy of Management Annals*, vol 6, pp 211-83.

Denis, J.-L., Lamonthe, L., Langley, A. and Valette, A. (1999) 'The struggle to redefine boundaries in health care systems', in D. Drock, M. Powell and C. Hinings (eds) *Restructuring the professional organisation*, London: Routledge, pp 105-30.

DH (Department of Health) (1998) *Partnership in action: New opportunities for joint working between health and social services*, London: DH.

DH (2013) *Integrated care: Our shared commitment*, London: DH.

Dickinson, H. (2014) *Performing governance: Partnerships, culture and New Labour*, Basingstoke: Palgrave Macmillan.

Dickinson, H. and Glasby, J. (2010) 'Why partnership working doesn't work', *Public Management Review*, vol 12, no 6, pp 811-28.

Dickinson, H. and O'Flynn, J. (2016) *Evaluating outcomes in health and social care* (2nd edn), Better Partnership Working series, Bristol: Policy Press.

Dickinson, H. and Sullivan, H. (2014) 'Towards a general theory of collaborative performance: The importance of efficacy and agency', *Public Administration*, vol 92, no 1, pp 161-77.

Dickinson, H., Bismark, M.M., Phelps, G. and Loh, E. (2015a) 'Future of medical engagement', *Australian Health Review*.

Dickinson, H., Freeman, T., Robinson, S. and Williams, I. (2011) 'Resource scarcity and priority-setting: from management to leadership in the rationing of health care?', *Public Money and Management*, vol 31, pp 363-70.

Dickinson, H., Ham, C., Snelling, I. and Spurgeon, P. (2013) *Are we there yet? Models of medical leadership and their effectiveness: An exploratory study, Final report*, NIHR Service Delivery and Organisation programme.

Dickinson, H., Bismark, M., Phelps, G., Loh, E., Morris, J. and Thomas, L. (2015b) *Engaging professionals in organisational governance: The case of doctors and their role in the leadership and management of health services*, Melbourne, VIC: Melbourne School of Government.

Dixon-Woods, M., Baker, R., Charles, K., Dawson, J., Jerzembek, G., Martin, G. et al (2014) 'Culture and behaviour in the English National Health Service: overview of lessons from a large multimethod study', *BMJ Quality & Safety*, vol 23, pp 106-15.

Dubrin, A. (2004) *Leadership: Research findings, practice and skills*, New York: Houghton Mifflin.

Dunleavy, P. (1991) *Democracy, bureaucracy and public choice*, New York: Harvester Wheatsheaf.

Easterling, D. and Millesen, J.L. (2012) 'Diversifying civic leadership: What it takes to move from "new faces" to adaptive problem solving', *National Civic Review*, vol 101, pp 20-6.

Edwards, G. (2011) 'Concepts of community: A framework for contextualizing distributed leadership', *International Journal of Management Reviews*, vol 13, pp 301-12.

Eggers, W. (2008) 'The changing nature of government: network governance', in J. O'Flynn and J. Wanna (eds) *Collaborative governance: A new era of public policy in Australia?*, Acton, ACT: ANU Press, pp 23-9 (http://press.anu.edu.au?p=96031).

Emery, F. and Trist, E. (1973) *Towards a social ecology*, New York: Plenum.

Evetts, J. (1999) 'Professionalisation and professionalism: issues for interprofessional care', *Journal of Interprofessional Care*, vol 13, pp 119-28.

Exworthy, M. and Powell, M. (2004) 'Big windows and little windows: implementation in the "congested state"', *Public Administration*, vol 82, pp 263-81.

Fawkes, S. (2012) *Leadership for systems change in preventive health: Review of the literature and current activity*, Melbourne, VIC: Victorian Government Department of Health.

Ferlie, E., Pettigrew, A., Ashburner, L. and Fitzgerald, L. (1996) *The new public management in action*, Oxford: Oxford University Press.

Ferlie, E., Fitzgerald, L., McGivern, G., Dopson, S. and Bennett, C. (2011) 'Public policy networks and "wicked problems": A nascent solution?', *Public Administration*, vol 89, no 2, pp 307-24.

Fiedler, F. (1967) *A theory of leadership effectiveness*, New York: McGraw-Hill.

Field, J. and Peck, E. (2003) 'Mergers and acquisitions in the private sector: what are the lessons for health and social services?', *Social Policy & Administration*, vol 37, pp 742-55.

Fitzgerald, L., Ferlie, E., Wood, M. and Hawkins, C. (1999) 'Evidence into practice: an exploratory analysis of the interpretation of evidence', in A. Mark and S. Dopson (eds) *Organisational behaviour in health care: The research agenda*, Basingstoke: Macmillan, pp 189-206.

Fitzgerald, L., Ferlie, E., McGivern, G. and Buchanan, D. (2013) 'Distributed leadership patterns and service improvement: Evidence and argument from English healthcare', *The Leadership Quarterly*, vol 24, pp 227-39.

Fleming, L. and Waguespack, D.M. (2007) 'Brokerage, boundary spanning, and leadership in open innovation communities', *Organization Science*, vol 18, pp 165-80.

Ford, J., Harding, N. and Learmonth, M. (2008) *Leadership as identity: Constructions and destructions*, Basingstoke: Palgrave Macmillan.

Foster-Fishman, P.G., Berkowitz, S.L., Lounsbury, D.W., Jacobson, S. and Allen, N.A. (2001) 'Building collaborative capacity in community coalitions: a review and integrative framework', *American Journal of Community Psychology*, vol 29, no 2, pp 241-61.

Francis, R. (2013) *Report of the Mid Staffordshire NHS Foundation Trust Public Inquiry – Volume 3: Present and future*, London: The Stationery Office (www.midstaffspublicinquiry.com/report).

Freeman, T. and Peck, E. (2007) 'Performing governance: a partnership board dramaturgy', *Public Administration*, vol 85, issue 4, pp 907-29.

Friend, J.K., Power, J.M. and Yewlett, C.J.L. (1974) *Public planning: The inter-corporate dimension*, London: Tavistock.

Fullan, M. (2001) *Leading in a culture of change*, San Francisco, CA: Jossey-Bass.

Fung, A. (2015) 'Putting the public back into governance: The challenges of citizen participation and its future', *Public Administration Review*, vol 75, pp 513-22.

Gemmill, G. and Oakley, J. (1992) 'Leadership: an alienating social myth?', *Human Relations*, vol 45, pp 113-29.

George, J. (2000) 'Emotions and leadership: the role of emotional intelligence', *Human Relations*, vol 53, pp 1027-55.

Giddens, A. (1984) *The constitution of society*, Cambridge: Polity.

Giddens, A. (1993) 'Structuration theory: past, present and future', in C. Bryant and D. Jary (eds) *Giddens' theory of structuration*, London: Routledge.

Glasby, J. and Dickinson, H. (2014a) *A-Z of interagency working*, Basingstoke: Palgrave Macmillan.

Glasby, J. and Dickinson, H. (2014b) *Partnership working in health and social care: What is integrated care and how can we deliver it?* (2nd edn), Better partnership working series, Bristol: Policy Press.

Glendinning, C., Hudson, B., Hardy, B. and Young. R. (2002) *National evaluation of notifications for the use of the Section 31 partnership flexibilities in the Health Act 1999: Final project report*, Leeds/Manchester: Nuffield Institute for Health/National Primary Care Research and Development Centre.

Glover, A.J. (1938) 'The incidence of tonsil-lectomy in school children', *Proceedings of the Royal Society of Medicine*, 27 May, pp 1219-36.

Goffman, E. (1974) *Frame analysis: An essay on the organization of experience*, London: Harper & Row.

Goldsmith, S. and Eggers, W. (2004) *Governing by network: The new shape of the public sector*, Washington, DC: Brookings Institute Press.

Goleman, D. (1996) *Emotional intelligence: Why it can matter more than IQ*, London: Bloomsbury.

Graeber, D. (2015) *The utopia of rules*, London: Melville House.

Greenhalgh, T., Robert, G., McFarlane, F., Bate, P. and Kyriakidou, O. (2004) 'Diffusion of innovations in service organizations: Systematic review and recommendations', *Milbank Quarterly*, vol 82, no 4, pp 581-629.

Grint, K. (2000) *The arts of leadership*, Oxford: Oxford University Press.

Grint, K. (2005a) 'Problems, problems, problems: the social construction of "leadership"', *Human Relations*, vol 58, pp 1467-94.

Grint, K. (2005b) *Leadership: Limits and possibilities*, Basingstoke: Palgrave Macmillan.

Gronn, P. (2002) 'Distributed leadership as a unit of analysis', *The Leadership Quarterly*, vol 13, pp 423-51.

Gronn, P. (2015) 'The view from inside leadership configurations', *Human Relations*, vol 68, pp 545-60.

Haines, M., Brown, B., Craig, J., d'Este, C., Elliott, E., Klineberg, E. et al (2012) 'Determinants of successful clinical networks: the conceptual framework and study protocol', *Implementation Science*, vol 7, no 16, pp 1-10.

Hajer, M.A. (2005) 'Rebuilding ground zero. The politics of performance', *Planning Theory and Practice*, vol 6, no 4, pp 445-64.

Hardacre, J. and Peck, E. (2005) 'What is organisational development?', in E. Peck (ed) *Organisational development in healthcare: Approaches, innovations, achievements*, Abingdon: Radcliffe Medical Publishing.

Hardy, B., Turrell, A. and Wistow, G. (1992) *Innovations in community care management*, Aldershot: Avebury.

Harrison, A., Hunter, D., Marnoch, G. and Pollitt, C. (1992) *Just managing: Power and culture in the NHS*, Basingstoke: Macmillan.

Hay, C. (1995) 'Structure and agency', in G. Stoker and D. Marsh (eds) *Theory and methods in political science*, London: Macmillan, pp 189-206.

Head, B. (2014) 'The collaboration solution? Factors for collaborative success', in J. O'Flynn, D. Blackman and J. Halligan (eds) *Crossing boundaries in public management and policy: The international experience*, Abingdon: Routledge, pp 142-57.

Heifetz, R., Grashow, A. and Linksy, M. (2009) *The practice of adaptive leadership: Tools and tactics for changing your organization and the world*, Boston, MA: Harvard Business Press.

Hemphill, L., McGreal, S., Berry, J. and Watson, S. (2006) 'Leadership, power and multisector urban: regeneration partnerships', *Urban Studies*, vol 43, pp 59-80.

Herranz, J. (2008) 'The multisectoral trilemma of network management', *Journal of Public Administration, Research and Theory*, vol 18, no 1, pp 1-31.

Hersey, P. and Blanchard, K. (1988) *Management of organisational behaviour: Utilizing human resources*, Englewood Cliffs, NJ: Prentice-Hall.

Hood, C. (1995) 'Contemporary public management: a new global paradigm', *Public Policy and Administration*, vol 10, pp 104-17.

Hosking, D. (1988) 'Organizing, leadership and skilful process', *Journal of Management Studies*, vol 25, pp 147-66.

Houghton, J., Neck, C. and Manz, C. (2003) 'Self-leadership and superleadership: The heart and art of creating shared leadership in teams', in J. Pearce and J. Conger (eds) *Shared leadership: Reframing the hows and why of leadership*, Thousand Oaks, CA: Sage, pp 123-40.

House, R. (1971) 'A path-goal theory of leader effectiveness', *Administrative Science Quarterly*, vol 16, pp 321-38.

Hudson, B. (2000) 'Inter-agency collaboration: a sceptical view', in A. Brechin, H. Brown and M. Eby (eds) *Critical practice in health and social care*, Milton Keynes: Open University Press, pp 253-74.

Hudson, B. (2004) 'Care trusts: a sceptical view', in J. Glasby and E. Peck (eds) *Care trusts: Partnership working in action*, Abingdon: Radcliffe Medical Press, pp 83-94.

Hudson, B., Exworthy, M. and Peckham, S. (1998) *The integration of localised and collaborative purchasing: A review of the literature and framework for analysis*, Leeds: Nuffield Institute for Health.

Hunt, J.G. and Dodge, G.E. (2001) 'Leadership déjà vu all over again', *The Leadership Quarterly*, vol 11, pp 435-58.

Hunter, D.L. (1996) 'The changing roles of health personnel in health and health care management', *Social Science & Medicine*, vol 43, pp 799-808.

Institute of Medicine (2001) *Crossing the quality chasm: A new health system for the 21st century*, Washington, DC: National Academy Press.

Jelphs, K., Dickinson, H. and Miller, R. (2016) *Working in teams*, Bristol: Policy Press.

Judge, W. and Ryman, J. (2001) 'The shared leadership challenge in strategic alliances: lessons from the US healthcare industry', *Academy of Management Executive*, vol 15, pp 71-9.

Jupp, B. (2000) *Working together: Creating a better environment for cross-sector partnerships*, London: Demos.

Kanter, R.M. (1989) *When giants learn to dance*, New York: Simon & Schuster.

Kanter, R.M. (1994) 'Collaborative advantage: the art of alliances', *Harvard Business Review*, vol 72, pp 96-108.

Katz, D. and Kahn, R.L. (1966) *Organizations and the system concept*, New York: Wiley.

Keast, R., Mandell, M.P., Brown, K. and Woolcock, G. (2004) 'Network structures: Working differently and changing expectations', *Public Administration Review*, vol 64, pp 363-71.

Kickert, W., Klijn, E.-H. and Koppenjan, J.F.M. (1997) *Managing complex networks: Strategies for the public sector*, London: Sage Publications.

Kingdon, J. (1995) *Agendas, alternatives and public policies*, Boston, MD: Little, Brown & Co.

Kitchener, M. (2002), 'Mobilizing the logic of managerialism in professional fields: The case of academic health centre mergers', *Organization Studies*, vol 23, no 3, pp 391-420.

Lambright, W.H. and Quinn, M.M. (2011) 'Understanding leadership in public administration: The biographical approach', *Public Administration Review*, vol 71, no 5, pp 782-90.

Laming, H. (2003) *The Victoria Climbié Inquiry: Report of an inquiry*, London: The Stationery Office.

Laming, W. (2009) *The protection of children in England: A progress report*, London: Department for Children, Schools and Families.

Lauchs, M.A., Keast, R.L. and Yousefpour, N. (2011) 'Corrupt police networks: uncovering hidden relationship patterns, functions and roles', *Policing and Society*, vol 21, no 1, pp 110-27.

Lawler, J. (2000) 'The rise of managerialism in social work', in E. Harlow and J. Lawler (eds) *Management, social work and change*, London: Ashgate.

Lawler, J. (2004) 'Meaning and being: existentialist concepts in leadership', *International Journal of Management Concepts and Philosophy*, vol 1, pp 61-72.

Leifer, R. and Delbecq, A. (1976) 'Organizational/environmental interchange: a model of boundary spanning activity', *Academy of Management Review*, January, pp 40-50.

Leutz, W. (1999) 'Five laws for integrating medical and social services: lessons from the United States and the United Kingdom', *The Milbank Quarterly*, vol 77, no 1, pp 77-110.

Likert, R. (1961) 'An emerging theory of organizations, leadership and management', in L. Petrullo and E. Bass (eds) *Leadership and interpersonal behaviour*, New York: Holt, Rinehart & Winston.

Ling, T. (2002) 'Delivering joined-up government in the UK: dimensions, issues and problems', *Public Administration*, vol 80, pp 615-42.

Lipsky, M. (1980) *Street-level bureaucracy: Dilemmas of the individual in public services*, New York: Basic Books.

Lowe, K.B. and Gardner, W.L. (2001) 'Ten years of the leadership quarterly: Contributions and challenges for the future', *The Leadership Quarterly*, vol 11, pp 459-14.

Lynn, L. (2006) *Public management. Old and new*, London: Routledge.

Mangham, I. (2004) 'Leadership and integrity', in J. Storey (ed) *Leadership in organisations: Key issues and trends*, Oxford: Routledge.

Mannion, R. and Davies, H.T.O. (2015) 'Cultures of silence and cultures of voice: The role of whistleblowing in healthcare organisations', *International Journal of Health Policy and Management*, vol 4, pp 503-5.

Marks, M.L. and Mirvis, P.H. (1992) 'Rebuilding after the merger: dealing with "survivor sickness"', *Organizational Dynamics*, pp 18-32.

Martin, G.P. and Learmonth, M. (2012) 'A critical account of the rise and spread of "leadership": the case of UK healthcare', *Social Science & Medicine*, vol 74, pp 281-8.

Martin, J. (1992) *Culture in organizations: Three perspectives*, Oxford: Oxford University Press.

Maslow, A. (1954) *Motivation and personality*, New York: Harper.

Matka, E., Barnes, M. and Sullivan, H. (2002) 'Health Action Zones: "creating alliances to achieve change"', *Policy Studies*, vol 23, pp 97-106.

McCallin, A.M. (2003) 'Interdisciplinary team leadership: A revisionist approach for an old problem?', *Journal of Nursing Management*, vol 11, pp 364-70.

McCray, J. and Ward, C. (2003) 'Editorial notes for November: leading interagency collaboration', *Journal of Nursing Management*, vol 11, pp 361-3.

McGregor, D. (1966) *Leadership and motivation*, Cambridge, MA: MIT Press.

McGuire, M. (2006) 'Collaborative public management: assessing what we know and how we know it', *Public Administration Review*, vol 66, pp 33-43.

Meyerson, D. and Martin, J. (1987) 'Cultural change: an integration of three different views', *Journal of Management Studies*, vol 24, pp 623-43.

Mintzberg, H. (1979) *The structuring of organisations: A synthesis of research*, Englewood Cliffs, NJ: Prentice-Hall.

Mintzberg, H. and van der Heyden, L. (1999) 'Organigraphs: drawing how companies really work', *Harvard Business Review*, vol 77, pp 87-94.

Mitchell, S.M. and Shortell, S.M. (2000) 'Governance and management of effective community health partnerships: a typology for research, policy and practice', *The Milbank Quarterly*, vol 78, pp 241-89.

National Sure Start Evaluation (2005) *Early impacts of Sure Start local programmes on children and families: Report of the cross-sectional study of 9-and 36-month old children and their families*, London: The Stationery Office.

Needham, C. (2011) *Personalising public services: Understanding the personalisation narrative*, Bristol: Policy Press.

Nelson, E., Batalden, P.B., Huber, T.P., Mohr, J.J., Godfrey, M.M., Headrick, L.A. and Wasson, J.H. (2002) 'Microsystems in health care: Part 1. Learning from high-performing front-line clinical units', *Journal on Quality Improvement*, vol 28, pp 472-93.

Newman, J. (2012) *Working the spaces of power: Activism, neoliberalism and gendered work*, London: Bloomsbury Academic.

Newman, J. (2013) 'Constituting context', in C. Pollitt (ed) *Context in public policy and management: The missing link?*, Cheltenham: Edward Elgar Publishing Ltd, pp 35-44.

NHS Future Forum (2012) *Integration: A report from the NHS Future Forum*, London: Future Forum.

Norman, I.J. and Peck, E. (1999) 'Working together in adult community mental health services: an inter-professional dialogue', *Journal of Mental Health*, vol 8, pp 217-30.

O'Leary, R., Gerard, C. and Bingham, L.B. (2006) 'Introduction to the symposium on collaborative public management', *Public Administration Review*, vol 66, pp 6-9.

O'Toole, L.J. (1998) 'The implications for democracy in a networked bureaucratic world', *Journal of Public Administration Research and Theory*, vol 7, pp 443-59.

O'Toole, L.J. and Meier, K.J. (2004) 'Desperately seeking Selznick: cooptation and the dark side of public management in networks', *Public Administration Review*, vol 64, pp 681-93.

ODPM (Office of the Deputy Prime Minister) (2005a) *A process evaluation of the negotiation of pilot local area agreements*, London: ODPM.

ODPM (2005b) *National evaluation of local strategic partnerships issues paper: Leadership in local strategic partnerships*, London: ODPM.

ODPM (2005c) *Evaluation of local strategic partnerships: Interim report*, London: ODPM.

ODPM (2007) *Evidence of savings, improved outcomes, and good practice attributed to local area agreements*, London: ODPM.

OECD (Organisation for Economic Co-operation and Development) (1995) *Governance in transition: Public management reforms in OECD countries*, Paris: OECD.

Oliver, A.L. and Ebers, M. (1998) 'Networking network studies: an analysis of conceptual configurations in the study of inter-organizational relationships', *Organization Studies*, vol 19, pp 549-83.

Oliver, P. and Johnston, H. (2000) 'What a good idea: frames and ideologies in social movements research', *Mobilization*, vol 5, no 1, pp 37-54.

Osborne, S. (2006) 'The new public governance?', *Public Management Review*, vol 8, pp 377-87.

Osborne, S. (ed) (2010) *The new public governance*, New York: Routledge.

Osborne, D. and Gaebler, T. (1993) *Reinventing government: How the entrepreneurial spirit is transforming the public sector*, London: Penguin Books.

Parker, M. (2000) *Organisational culture and identity*, London: Sage Publications.

Payne, M. (2000) *Teamwork in multiprofessional care*, Basingstoke: Macmillan.

Peck, E. (2002) 'Integrating health and social care', *Managing Community Care*, vol 10, no 3, pp 16-19.

Peck, E. and 6, P. (2006) *Beyond delivery: Policy implementation as sense-making and settlement*, Basingstoke: Palgrave.

Peck, E. and Crawford, A. (2004) *'Culture' in partnerships: What do we mean by it and what can we do about it?*, Leeds: Integrated Care Network.

Peck, E. and Dickinson, H. (2008) 'Managing integration: partnership working and organisational culture', in J. Glasby and H. Dickinson (eds) *International health and social care: Partnership working in action*, Oxford: Blackwell Publishing, pp 10-26.

Peck, E. and Dickinson, H. (2009) *Performing leadership*, Basingstoke: Palgrave Macmillan.

Peck, E. and Dickinson, H. (2010) 'Pursuing legitimacy: conceptualising and developing leaders' performances', *Leadership & Organization Development Journal*, vol 31, no 7, pp 630-42.

Peck, E., Gulliver, P. and Towell, D. (2002) *Modernising partnerships: An evaluation of Somerset's innovations in the commissioning and organisation of Mental Health Services*, London: Institute of Applied Health and Social Policy, King's College.

Peck, E., Towell, D. and Gulliver, P. (2001) 'The meanings of "culture" in health and social care: a case study of the combined trust in Somerset', *Journal of Interprofessional Care*, vol 15, pp 319-27.

Peck, E., 6, P., Gulliver, P. and Towell, D. (2004) 'Why do we keep meeting like this? The board as ritual in health and social care', *Health Services Management Research*, vol 17, pp 100-9.

Peters, T.J. and Waterman, R.H. (1982) *In search of excellence: Lessons from America's best-run companies*, New York: Harper & Row.

Pettigrew, A., Ferlie, E.B. and McKee, L. (1992) *Shaping strategic change. Making change in large organisations: The case of the National Health Service*, London: Sage Publications.

Pierre, J. and Peters, B.G. (2000) *Governance, politics and the state*, New York: St Martin's Press.

PIU (Performance and Innovation Unit) (2001) *Strengthening leadership in the public sector*, London: Cabinet Office Strategy Unit.

Pollitt, C. (1993) *Managerialism and the public services: The Anglo-American experience*, Oxford: Blackwell.

Pollitt, C. (2000) 'Is the emperor in his underwear? An analysis of the impacts of public management reform', *Public Management*, vol 2, pp 181-99.

Porteous, P. (2013) 'Localism: from adaptive to social leadership', *Policy Studies*, vol 34, pp 523-40.

Powell, M. and Moon, G. (2001) 'Health Action Zones: the "third way" of a new area-based policy', *Health and Social Care in the Community*, vol 9, pp 43-50.

Pye, A. (1995) 'Strategy through dialogue and doing: a game of Mornington Crescent?', *Management Learning*, vol 25, pp 445-62.

Pye, A. (2005) 'Leadership and organizing: sensemaking in action', *Leadership*, vol 1, pp 31-50.

Rafferty, A., Philoppou, J., Fitzpatrick, J. and Ball, J. (2015) *'Culture of care' barometer*, London: King's College.

Rhodes, R.A.W. (1996) 'The new governance: governing without government', *Political Studies*, vol 44, no 4, pp 652-67.

Rhodes, R.A.W. (1997) *Understanding governance*, Buckingham and Philadelphia, PA: Open University Press.

Rhodes, R.A.W. (2007) 'Understanding governance: Ten years on', *Organization Studies*, vol 28, pp 1243-64.

Rhodes, R.A.W. (2014) 'Recovering the "craft" of public administration in network governance', Pleanary address to the International Political Science Association World Congress, Montreal, 19-24 July (www.wa.ipaa.org.au/content/docs/IPAA2014/Rhodes%202014%20 IPAA%20version.pdf).

Robertson, P.J. (1995) 'Involvement in boundary-spanning activity: mitigating the relationship between work setting and behaviour', *Journal of Public Administration Research and Theory*, vol 5, pp 73-98.

Rodríguez, C., Langley, A., Beland, F. and Denis, J.-L. (2007) 'Governance, power, and mandated collaboration in an interorganizational network', *Administration & Society*, vol 39, no 2, pp 150-93.

Rugkåsa, J., Shortt, N. and Boydell, L. (2007) 'The right tool for the task: "boundary spanners" in a partnership approach to tackle fuel poverty in rural Northern Ireland', *Health and Social Care in the Community*, vol 15, pp 221-30.

Rummery, K. and Glendinning, C. (2000) *Primary care and social services: Developing new partnerships for older people*, Abingdon: Radcliffe Medical Press.

Russell, H. et al (2010) *The role of local strategic partnerships and local area agreements in promoting equalities*, EHRC Research Report 63, Manchester: Equalities and Human Rights Commission.

Salovey, P. and Mayer, J. (1990) 'Emotional intelligence', *Imagination, Cognition and Personality*, vol 9, pp 185-211.

Sarason, S.B. and Lorentz, E.M. (1998) *Crossing boundaries: Collaboration, coordination and the redefinition of resources*, San Francisco, CA: Jossey-Bass.

Schechner, R. (2003) *Performance studies: An introduction*, London: Routledge.

Schön, D.A. and Rein, M. (1994) *Frame reflection: Toward the resolution of intractable policy controversies*, New York: Basic Books.

Scott, T., Mannion, R., Davies, H.T.O. and Marshall, M. (2003a) *Healthcare performance and organisational culture*, Abingdon: Radcliffe Medical Press.

Scott, T., Mannion, R., Davies, H.T.O. and Marshall, M. (2003b) 'The quantitative measurement of organisational culture in health care: a review of the available instruments', *Health Services Research*, vol 38, pp 923-45.

Secretary of State for Health (2013) *Patients first and foremost: The initial government response to the report of the Mid Staffordshire NHS Foundation Trust public inquiry*, London: The Stationery Office.

Sermeus, W., Vanheacht, K. and Vleugels, A. (2001) 'The Belgian–Dutch clinical pathway network', *Journal of Integrated Care Pathways*, vol 5, pp 10-14.

Shirley, J. (2000) 'Clinical governance in an independent hospital', *Clinician in Management*, vol 9, pp 229-33.

Skelcher, C. (2000) 'Changing images of the state: overloaded, hollowed out, congested', *Public Policy & Administration*, vol 15, pp 3-19.

Smith, K. (2014) *Beyond evidence-based policy in public health*, Basingstoke: Palgrave Macmillan.

Snebold, L. (2015) 'Public health transformation: Helping local health departments navigate change through adaptive leadership', *Journal of Public Health Management and Practice*, vol 21, pp 310-12.

Spillane, J. and Diamond, J. (2007) *Distributed leadership in practice*, Critical Issues in Educational Leadership Series, New York: Teachers College, Columbia University.

Spurgeon, P., Clark, J. and Ham, C. (2011) *Medical leadership: From the dark side to centre stage*, London: Radcliffe Publishing Limited.

Stacey, R. (1999) *Strategic management and organisational dynamics: The challenge of complexity*, London: *Financial Times*.

Stern, R. and Green, J. (2005) 'Boundary workers and the management of frustration: a case study of two Healthy City partnerships', *Health Promotion International*, vol 20, pp 269-76.

Storey, J. (2004a) 'Signs of change: "damned rascals and beyond"', in J. Storey (ed) *Leadership in organisations: Key issues and trends*, Oxford: Routledge.

Storey, J. (2004b) 'Changing theories of leadership and leadership development', in J. Storey (ed) *Leadership in organisations: Key issues and trends*, Oxford: Routledge.

Sullivan, H. (2014) 'Collaboration as the new normal? Global trends, public policy and everyday practice', Keynote speech delivered at the Policy & Politics Conference, 17 September, Bristol (www.icpublicpolicy.org/conference/file/reponse/1433928999.pdf).

Sullivan, H. and Skelcher, C. (2002) *Working across boundaries: Collaboration in public services*, Basingstoke: Palgrave.

Sullivan, H., Judge, K. and Sewel, K. (2004) '"In the eye of the beholder": perceptions of local impact in English Health Action Zones', *Social Science & Medicine*, vol 59, pp 1603-12.

Sullivan, H., Williams, P. and Jeffares, S. (2012) 'Leadership for collaboration', *Public Management Review*, vol 14, no 1, pp 41-66.

Sweeney, K. (2005) 'Emergence, complexity and organisational development', in E. Peck (ed) *Organisational development in healthcare: Approaches, innovations, achievements*, Abingdon: Radcliffe Medical Publishing, pp 143-66.

Thomas, H. (2003) 'Clinical networks for doctors and managers', *British Medical Journal*, vol 326, no 7390, p 655.

Thompson, G. (1991) 'Comparison between models', in G. Thompson, J. Mitchell, R. Levacic and J. Francis (eds) *Markets, hierarchies and networks: The coordination of social life*, London: Sage Publications, pp 243-5.

Thompson, J.D. (1967) *Organizations in action: Social science bases of administrative theory*, New York: McGraw-Hill.

Tuch, C. and O'Sullivan, N. (2007) 'The impact of acquisitions on firm performance: A review of the evidence', *International Journal of Management Reviews*, vol 9, issue 2, pp 141-70.

Uhl-Bien, M. (2006) 'Relational leadership theory: Exploring the social processes of leadership and organizing', *The Leadership Quarterly*, vol 17, pp 654-76.

University of East Anglia (2007) *Children's trust pathfinders: Innovative partnerships for improving the well-being of children and young people*, Norwich: University of East Anglia in Association with the National Children's Bureau.

van Wart, M. (2003) 'Public-sector leadership theory: An assessment', *Public Administration Review*, vol 63, no 2, pp 214-28.

Vangen, S. and Huxham, C. (2003) 'Enacting leadership for collaborative advantage: dilemmas of ideology and pragmatism in the activities of partnership managers', *British Journal of Management*, vol 14, pp 61-76.

Vogel, R. and Masal, D. (2015) 'Public leadership: A review of the literature and framework for future research', *Public Management Review*, vol 17, no 8, pp 1165-89.

Volkoff, O., Chan, Y.E. and Newson, P.E.F. (1999) 'Leading the development and implementation of collaborative interorganizational systems', *Information and Management*, vol 35, pp 63-75.

Vroom, V. and Jago, A. (1988) *The new leadership: Managing participation in organisations*, Englewood Cliffs, NJ: Prentice-Hall.

Vroom, V. and Yetton, P. (1973) *Leadership and decision-making*, Pittsburgh, PA: University of Pittsburgh Press.

Warner, M., Gould, N. and Jones, A. (2003) 'Community Health Alliances through Integrated Networks (CHAIN). Reporting project progress in South Wales with reference to the National Service Framework for older people', Paper presented to the IJIC/WHO 3rd International Conference on Integrated Care, Barcelona, February.

Weick, K. (1995) *Sensemaking in organizations*, London: Sage Publications.

Weiss, E.S., Anderson, R.M. and Lasker, R.D. (2002) 'Making the most of collaboration: exploring the relationship between partnership synergy and partnership functioning', *Health Education and Behaviour*, vol 29, pp 683-98.

Welsh Assembly Government (2011) *Sustainable social services for Wales: A framework for action*, Cardiff: Welsh Assembly Government.

Wennberg, J.E., Roos, N. and Sola, L. (1987) 'Use of claims data systems to evaluate health care outcomes: mortality and reoperation following prostatectomy', *Journal of the American Medical Association*, vol 257, pp 933-6.

West, M., Eckert, R., Steward, K. and Pasmore, B. (2014) *Developing collective leadership for health care*, London: The King's Fund.

Wheatley, M. (2001) *Leadership and the new science*, San Francisco, CA: Berrett-Koehler.

Williams, P. (2002) 'The competent boundary spanner', *Public Administration*, vol 80, pp 103-24.

Williams, P. (2005) 'Collaborative capability and the management of interdependencies: the contribution of boundary spanners', Unpublished PhD thesis, University of Bristol.

Williams, P. (2012) *Collaboration in public policy and practice: Perspectives on boundary spanners*, Bristol: Policy Press.

Wistow, G. and Waddington, E. (2006) 'Learning from doing: implications of the Barking and Dagenham experiences for integrating health and social care', *Journal of Integrated Care*, vol 14, pp 8-18.

Zaleznik, A. (1992) 'Managers and leaders: are they different?', *Harvard Business Review*, vol 3, pp 126-38.

Zimmerman, B.J., Lindberg, C. and Plsek, P.E. (1998) *Edgeware: Insights from complexity science for health care leaders*, Dallas, TX: VHA Publishing.

Zollo, M. and Meier, D. (2008) 'What is M&A performance?', *The Academy of Management Perspectives*, vol 22, no 3, pp 55-77.

Index